SOCIETY
OF BIBLICAL
LITERATURE

DISSERTATION SERIES
J. J. M. Roberts, Old Testament Editor
Charles Talbert, New Testament Editor

Number 94
THE CONFESSIONS OF JEREMIAH:
THEIR INTERPRETATION AND ROLE IN CHAPTERS 1–25
. by
Kathleen M. O'Connor

Kathleen M. O'Connor

THE CONFESSIONS OF JEREMIAH: THEIR INTERPRETATION AND ROLE IN CHAPTERS 1-25

Scholars Press
Atlanta, Georgia

THE CONFESSIONS OF JEREMIAH: THEIR INTERPRETATION AND ROLE IN CHAPTERS 1-25

Kathleen M. O'Connor

Ph.D., 1984
Princeton Theological Seminary

Advisor:
J. J. M. Roberts

Library of Congress Cataloging-in-Publication Data

O'Connor, Kathleen M., 1942–
The confessions of Jeremiah.

(Dissertation series / Society of Biblical
Literature ; no. 94)
Bibliography: p.
1. Bible. O.T. Jeremiah I–XXV – Criticism,
interpretation, etc. 2. Jeremiah (Biblical prophet)
I. Title. II. Series: Dissertation series
(Society of Biblical Literature) ; no. 94.
BS1525.2.O36 1988   224'.206   86-29803
ISBN: 1-55540-000-0 (alk. paper)
ISBN: 1-55540-001-9 (pbk.: alk. paper)

Printed in the United States of America

Contents

vi

Acknowledgments

A dissertation is a personal suffering and a private exuberance, but it comes to life only in an intricate web of human relationships. To all those who have nurtured it and me, I give thanks:

To the Sisters of Saint Dominic, Newburgh, New York, for creating a climate that fostered the intellectual life and for their love and trust even as I left them to follow a different life.

To Thomas Aquinas Collins, O.P., the moving spirit of Biblical Studies at Providence College, for "setting me on a rock too high for me to reach" and "for staying in the wings" ever since.

To Bernard W. Anderson, Professor Emeritus of Old Testament Theology, for the inspiration of his masterful teaching and writing, for the privilege of assisting him in the classroom, for specific suggestions regarding Jeremiah, and above all, for encouraging my biblical and theological interests from the very first.

To the director of this dissertation, Jimmy Jack McBee Roberts, William Henry Green Professor of Old Testament Literature, for vigilant attention to the details of this study, for ready availability for consultation, for good-humored support that both challenged and encouraged me and for the example of his own insightful and exacting scholarship.

To Katharine Doob Sakenfeld, Associate Professor of Old Testament, for advice and inspiration in matters biblical and human.

To the community of Faculty and Ph.D. women at Princeton Seminary for their sense of sisterhood in scholarship and church.

To my many friends old and new, especially Ben Ollenburger for much instruction, and to both Ben and Elizabeth Gaines for shared laughter and tears in the challenges of life and work, and now, to Renate Craine for honesty, love and support.

To all my family for their long-suffering love through my lamentations.
To my typist, Jim Griesmer, one of the greatest blessings to come to me
in the process of this study, for love and generosity surpassing all.

Ossining, New York
March 1984

Abbreviations

AB	Anchor Bible
AHW	W. von Soden, *Akkadisches Handworterbuch*
AJSLL	*American Journal of Semitic Languages and Literature*
AnThRev	*Anglican Theological Review*
ATD	Das Alte Testament Deutsch
BB	Biblische Beiträge
BDB	F. Brown, S. R. Driver and C. A. Briggs, *Hebrew and English Lexicon of the Old Testament*
BHS	*Biblia Hebraica Stuttgartensia*
Bib	*Biblica*
Bib Leb	*Bibel und Leben*
BKAT	Biblischer Kommentar: Altes Testament
BST	Basel Studies of Theology
BZAW	Beihefte zur *ZAW*
CBC	Cambridge Bible Commentary
CBQ	*Catholic Biblical Quarterly*
CTM	Calwer Theologische Monographien
EvT	*Evangelische Theologie*
FB	Forschung zur Bibel
FRLANT	Forschungen zur Religion und Literatur des Alten und Neuen Testaments
GKC	*Gesenius' Hebrew Grammar*, ed. E. Kautzsch, tr. A. E. Cowley
GUOST	*Glasgow University Oriental Society Transactions*
HAT	Handbuch zum Alten Testament
Herm	Hermeneia
HKAT	Handkommentar zum Alten Testament

HSM	Harvard Semitic Monographs
HUCA	*Hebrew Union College Annual*
IB	*Interpreter's Bible*
IDB	G. A. Buttrick, ed., *Interpreter's Dictionary of the Bible*
Int	*Interpretation*
JBL	*Journal of Biblical Literature*
JJS	*Journal of Jewish Studies*
JNES	*Journal of Near Eastern Studies*
JPS	The Jewish Publication Society of America Translation
JSS	*Journal of Semitic Studies*
JTS	*Journal of Theological Studies*
KHAT	Kurzer Hand-Kommentar zum Alten Testament
KAT	Kommentar zum Alten Testament
MT	Masoretic Text
Misc BibOr	*Miscellanea Biblia et Orientalia*
NCCHS	Nelson Catholic Commentary on Holy Scripture
OTL	Old Testament Library
PCB	*Peake's Commentary on the Bible*
RB	*Revue Biblique*
RechSciRel	*Recherches de Science Religieuse*
RevScRel	*Revue des Sciences Religieuses*
RHPR	*Revue d'Histoire et de Philosophie religieuses*
RSV	*Revised Standard Version*
SGVSGTR	Sammlung Gemeinverständlicher Vorträge und Schriften aus dem Gebiet der Theologie und Religionsgeschichte
SBLDS	Society of Biblical Literature Dissertation Series
SBT	Studies in Biblical Theology
SEAJT	*South East Asia Journal of Theology*
TBu	Theologische Bücherei
ThRu	*Theologische Rundschau*
TLZ	*Theologische Literaturzeitung*
UF	*Ugarit-Forschungen*
VD	*Verbum Domini*
VT	*Vetus Testamentum*
VTS	Vetus Testamentum Supplements

Introduction

The five poems of Jeremiah generally known as the confessions (11:18-12:6; 15:10-21; 17:14-18; 18:18-23; 20:7-18) are the source of Jeremiah's reputation as a less than perfect prophet. Laced with cries of anger, groans of self-pity and pleas for retaliation against his enemies, these poetic pieces create the impression that Jeremiah was a man of small vision and narrow self-centeredness. They voice resistance to his prophetic vocation and question the justice of the God who called him to a life of prophecy.

Some scholars take comfort in this display of human weakness.[1] If the prophet can be so frail, all the more so the average believer. Others see the intrusion of the personal as an indication of prophecy's decline in Israel.[2] No longer is the divine word presented in pure form; in Jeremiah's confessions, it becomes inextricably mixed with the human. Still others deny the personal voice in the confessions by interpreting them as the cries of the community expressing itself through the corporate symbol of the prophet.[3]

---

[1]See, for example, William Holladay, *Jeremiah: Spokesman Out Of Time* (Philadelphia: Pilgrim Press Book from United Church Press, 1974) 12, 144; J. A. Thompson, *The Book of Jeremiah* (Grand Rapids: William B. Eerdmans, 1980), 88-92; E. W. Nicholson, *Jeremiah 1-25*, CBC (Cambridge: University Press, 1973) 114.

[2]Gerhard von Rad, "Die Konfessionen Jeremias," *EvT* 3 (1936) 265-276, was the first to articulate this view.

[3]Henning Graf Reventlow, *Liturgie und prophetisches Ich bei Jeremia* (Gütersloh: Gerd Mohn, 1963); Erhard Gerstenberger, "Jeremiah's Complaints. Observations on Jer 15:10-21," *JBL* 82/4 (1963) 393-408; A. H. J. Gunneweg, "Konfession oder Interpretation im Jeremiabuch," *ZTK* 67/4 (1970) 395-416; Robert P. Carroll, *From Chaos to Covenant: Prophecy in the Book of Jeremiah* (New York: Crossroad, 1981) 107-130.

The confessions' expressions of abrupt vacillations in mood give the appearance not only of psychological disorder within the prophet but also of textual displacement within the poems. The confessions' chaotic appearance in the Masoretic Text has so unsettled exegetes and translators that they have resorted to amputation. As a way of supplying the poems with more logical structures, translators of critical English versions, The New English Bible,[4] The New American Bible,[5] The Jerusalem Bible[6] and the Anchor Bible Commentary[7] have emended the texts radically. They eliminate and rearrange words and verses seemingly at will. However, their scholarly consensus does not extend to the criteria underlying their emendations. As a result, no common view informs decisions about what should be changed or upon what grounds the changes should be made.

On the basis of the poems' personal character, many scholars have concluded that the motivation for their preservation and collection derived from biographical interest in the prophet.[8] But no other prophetic material was preserved for biographical purposes; even the marriage problems of Hosea served a public, prophetic intention. The anachronistic nature of this biographical criterion alone whould arouse suspicion about its validity.

It is not only the personal voice of the confessions which makes them anomalous in prophetic literature. They intrude upon the Book of Jeremiah with disturbing suddenness, apparently without connection to the materials around them. This feature of the poems has contributed to the general scholarly perception of the Book as a haphazard collection of materials with little logical arrangement other than, perhaps, that of chronology.[9] Scholars understand this Book, along with the others in the

---

[4]15:13-14 are eliminated.

[5]11:19-23 is placed after 12:1-6.

[6]12:6 is positioned after 11:18.

[7]John Bright, Jeremiah, AB (Garden City: Doubleday, 1965) places 12:6 before 11:18-23 and eliminates 15:12-14.

[8]See G. M. Behler, Les Confessions de Jeremie (Tournai: Casterman, 1959), preface; Nicholson, CBC, 112-114; Walter Baumgartner, Die Klagegedichte des Jeremia, BZAW 32 (Giessen: A. Töpelmann, 1917) 86; John Maclennan Berridge, Prophet, People and the Word of Yahweh: An Examination of Form in the Proclamation of the Prophet Jeremiah, BST 4 (Zurich: EVZ, 1970).

[9]For example, see Albert Condamin, Le Livre de Jeremie (Paris: J. Gabalda, 1920) XXII-XXIV; Friedrich Giesebrecht, Das Buch Jeremia,

prophetic cannon, to be compiled through the exclusive operation of principles of oral transmission. In their view, the Book lacks any evidence of purposeful literary editing.

This dissertation challenges these prevailing interpretations of the prophet, the confessions and the Book. It establishes that Jeremiah's use of the personal voice in the confessions does not provide evidence of a petulant and disturbed personality. Instead, the personal voice is a weapon in his battle for acceptance as a true prophet of Yahweh. Contrary to the usual view of them, the confessions served a public prophetic function in the original life setting of the prophet.

It demonstrates that the texts of the confessions are generally correct as they now stand in the MT. On form-critical grounds, it claims that the sharp changes in the prophet's moods can be explained by the confessions' literary form, the psalm of individual lament.[10] It presents a portrait of Jeremiah at variance with the prevailing one. Rather than viewing him as a voice of crescendoing despair, this study sees Jeremiah as a poet of Yahweh's praises. His confessions move from uncertainty and doubt to clarity of purpose in his vocation and confident trust in Yahweh.

On the basis of a redaction-critical analysis of cc 1-25, this investigation argues that the incorporation of the confessions into the Book was not a chance event but a purposeful literary editing. They are situated exclusively in cc 11-20 for literary and theological reasons.

What distinguishes this investigation from other studies of Jeremiah is both its focus and its combination of methodologies. Most studies of the confessions analyze them as isolated poems without regard to literary context.[11] This results from the presupposition that there is no

---

HAT (Göttingen: Vandenhoeck & Ruprecht, 1894) XV-XVII; Bernhard Duhm, *Das Buch Jeremia,* HKAT XI (Tübingen: J. C. B. Mohr, 1901) XVI.

[10]Against the view of the recently published work of Ferdinand Ahuis, *Der Klagende Gerichtsprophet: Studien zur Klage in der Überlieferung von den alttestamentlichen Gerichtspropheten,* CTM 12 (Stuttgart: Calwer, 1982) who understands the confessions as a mixture of forms. Because this book was received only after the completion of the present manuscript, it is cited infrequently. However, Ahuis' view is based on an improper delimitation of the poems. He divides the last confession into four unrelated components: 20:7-9; 10-12; 13; 14-18. He finds unwarranted redactional additions in 18:18-23. In addition, his application of forms to the confessions requires artificial interpretation of content to fit his categories. See especially pp. 30-31 and 77-113.

[11]See Baumgartner, *Die Klagegedichte;* Behler, *Les Confessions;*

connection between confession and context. Redaction-critical studies of
the Book, on the other hand, tend either to ignore the confessions or to
misinterpret them, missing both their role in the Book and the redactional
structure of the Book of which they form a part.[12]
    To avoid these perils, this study begins with an exegetical analysis of
each of the five confessions. The exegetical part of the dissertation, the
first five chapters, employs the methods of rhetorical-criticism and form-
criticism to uncover the structure, coherence and form of each confession
and to provide clues to their original purpose. Because Chapters 1 to 5 are
necessarily technically detailed studies, some readers may prefer to read
Chapters 6 through 9 first. The latter chapters draw conclusions from the
exegesis of Chapters 1 to 5 and then turn to the broader matters of redaction criticism.
    In Chapter 6, the study analyzes the confessions as a collection of
poems. Investigating their relationships to one another, it draws further
conclusions regarding their original purpose, arguments which derive from
the confessions' literary form, their use of covenant language and their
theological claims. It shows that the confessions legitimate Jeremiah
against the false prophets, and it provides a theoretical setting in the
prophet's life for their original proclamation. Chapter 7 investigates the
relationship of the confessions to their contexts and asks about the purpose for their inclusion in the Book. Chapter 8 analyzes the structure of
cc 1-25 and proposes that its loose literary and theological argument is
the literary creation of the Prose Writer.
    This study, therefore, has narrow boundaries. It is not the intention of
this writer to prepare a commentary on any part of the Book of Jeremiah
nor to present a redactional analysis of the entire Book. Nor does this

---

Franz D. Hubmann, *Untersuchungen zu den Konfession: Jer 11:18-12:6 und
Jer 15:10-21*, FB 30 (Echter, 1978); Norbert Ittmann, *Die Konfessionen
Jeremias: Ihre Bedeutung für die Verkündigung des Propheten*, WMANT 54
(Neukirchen-Vluyn: Neukirchener, 1981).
    [12]Winfried Thiel, *Die deuteronomistiche Redaktion von Jeremia 1-25*,
I, WMANT 41 (Neukirchen-Vluyn: Neukirchener, 1971); E. W. Nicholson,
*Preaching to the Exiles: A Study of the Prose Tradition of the Book of
Jeremiah* (New York: Schocken, 1970). Though a traditions-critical
investigation, this book overlooks the importance of the Confessions in
the text's final shape. See also Carroll, *From Chaos*. Unfortunately, Franz
Hubmann's study, "Stationen einer Berufung: Die Konfessionen Jeremias,"
Theologisch-praktische Quartalschrift I (1984) 25-39, arrived after the
completion of this study.

study resolve the baffling compositional problems of the Jeremianic corpus, though it does address them. The purpose of this study is to interpret the confessions and to discover their place in the Book. The confessions, therefore, serve as the lens through which the Book and many of its problems are viewed.

1

The First Confession: Jer 11:18–12:6

TRANSLATION

11:18   [1]Yahweh informed[2] me and I knew[3]
Then you showed[4] me their deeds.

11:19   But I was like a trusting lamb led to the slaughter.
I did not realize it was against me they plotted their schemes.
"Let us destroy the tree with its fruit,[5]
and let us cut him off from the land of the living that his name
may be remembered no more."

11:20   [6] Yahweh[7], Righteous Judge, Tester of heart and mind,
Let me see your vengeance upon them
for unto you I have revealed [8] my case.[9]

11:21   Therefore, thus says Yahweh, concerning the men of Anathoth
who seek my[10] life saying, "'Do not prophesy in the name of Yahweh, otherwise[11] you will die by our hands':[12]

11:22   [13]Behold, I am about to punish them. Their young men[14] will die
by the sword and their sons and their daughters will die by famine.

11:23   And they will have no remnant because I will bring evil upon the
men of Anathoth, the year of their punishment."

12:1   Innocent are you, Yahweh, if I make a claim against you.[15]
       Yet I want to present charges against you.
       Why does the way of the wicked prosper
       and all those who commit treachery flourish?

12:2   You have planted them and they have even taken root.
       They grow.[16] They bear fruit.
       You are near in their mouths
       but far from their hearts.

12:3   Yahweh, you know me,[17]
       You tested my mind with you.[18]
       [19]Separate them like sheep for the slaughter and
       consecrate them for the day of sacrifice.

12:4   How long will the land mourn [20]
       and the plants of every field wither because of the evil of
           those
       who inhabit it?
       The beasts and the birds are swept [21] away
       because they (the inhabitants) say, "He does not see our
           ways."[22]

12:5   If you run with footmen and they weary you,
       how will you compete with horses?
       And if in a land of peace you are careless,[23]
       how will you do in the thicket of the Jordan?

12:6   For even your brothers and the house of your father,
       even they have dealt treacherously with you,
       even they are in full cry after you.[24]
       Do not believe them though they speak well to you.

TEXT-CRITICAL NOTES

11:18   [1] וֹ is lacking in the LXX.

        [2] הוֹדִיעַנִי Some emend to הוֹדִיעֵנִי to follow the LXX, but
        the perfect gives a smoother sense.

3 וָאֵדְעָה Rudolph's emendation to וָאֵדְעֶךָ, (I knew it), *Jeremia*, 80, is unnecessary.

4 הֹרְאִיתַנִי The LXX reads רָאִיתִי. Bright, *Jeremiah*, AB 21 (Garden City: Doubleday, 1965), 84, n. g. follows the LXX on the grounds that the MT makes no sense without direct address to Yahweh. Direct address is implied here, however, which makes emendation unnecessary.

11:19   5 נַשְׁחִיתָה עֵץ בְּלַחְמוֹ The LXX reads Δεῦτε καὶ ἐμβάλωμεν ξύλον εἰς τὸν ἄρτον (Come let us put wood into his bread.) The difficulty arises from attempts to accommodate the verb to the supposed translation of the noun בלחמו. Some scholars have read the verb נשׁלכה; others emend to נשׁיתה. בלחמו, however, may mean "in its sap" or "in its youth" from לחח, "make moist," from the Akkadian *laḫu* (see von Soden *AHW*, I, 529), or the Ethiopic *laḫleḥa*, "be soft" (K.B. 499). Dahood, in "Hebrew-Ugaritic Lexicography IV," *Bib* 47 (1966), 409, suggests that בלחמו is לֶח with the enclitic mem and suffix. A. Guillaume proposed the Arabic cognate, לחם, "sap or "pulp," in *Prophecy and Divination* and, cf., James Muilenburg, unpublished commentary, "Jeremiah," Speer Library, Princeton Theological Seminary, Princeton, New Jersey, no date and no page numbers. Here יחם is taken simply as the bread or fruit of the tree.

11:20   6 ו is lacking in the LXX.

7 צבאות is deleted following the LXX. J. Gerald Janzen has argued persuasively that this epithet of the MT is frequently an expansion of the more original LXX, *Studies in the Text of Jeremiah* (Cambridge: Harvard University, 1973), 75. Janzen's argument is based upon the observation that the epithet appears frequently in the literature of the Alexandrian canon and, as a result, its absence in the LXX cannot be the result of Alexandrian community practice, but neither is its absence due to the translator's bias since it is included ten times in Jeremiah.

8 גִּלִּיתִי Some read גליתי, the piel infinitive construct of גלה or the Qal perfect, first common singular of גלל, "to roll," but the text is clear as it stands and is supported by the LXX.

[9]See Chapter 1 for a discussion of 11:20, a proposed doublet of 20:12.

11:21   [10] נַפְשֶׁךָ is emended to נפשׁי following the LXX. Jeremiah is the speaker.

[11] . . . וְלֹא is understood as a negative final clause, GKC 109g. The LXX reads εἰ δὲ μή.

[12] בְּיָדֵנוּ is emended to בידינו to follow the LXX.

11:22   [13] לכו . . . צבאות is omitted following the LXX. Janzen, *Studies*, 85, has demonstrated, against Bright, AB, 84, that הנה with the participle occur frequently in Jeremiah without the introductory formula. Moreover, most of this formula appears in v. 21 and is unnecessary here.

[14] הַבַּחוּרִים has been judged repetitive by Rudolph, *Jeremia*, 82, seeming to repeat the same category of people which appears next, i.e., "their sons." Both Rudolph and Muilenburg propose that הבחורים was added by dittography with בֶּחָרֶב. William Holladay, *The Architecture of Jer 1-20* (Lewisburg: Bucknell University and London: Associated University Presses, 1976) 139, suggests instead that הבחרים was added under the influence of 16:1-9. Since there is no textual evidence for the deletion of either of these words הבחורים should probably be understood as warriors, distinct from younger male and female children.

12:1   [15]Following the JPS.

12:2   [16]The LXX reads ἐτεκνοποίησαν (they bore children). Some have suggested ילדו or ילחו but the text is fine as it stands. See Hos 14:7 for a similar use of חלך.

12:3   [17] תְּרָאֵנִי is omitted here. It is lacking in the LXX. Althouth it is found in some of the Greek versions (see *Septuaginta: Vetus Testamentum Graecum auctoritate Societatis Gottingensis editum*), it disrupts the meter and creates an awkward Hebrew construction of an imperfect between two perfects.

[18]The JPS translates the line "You have tested my heart and found it with you." This loose translation emphasizes Jeremiah's innocence.

[19] לנבחה . . . התקם is lacking in the LXX but is found in some versions (see the Göttingen edition). It may have dropped out through homoeoteleuton, ה . . . . ה.

12:4

[20] תאבל can mean both "to mourn" and "to wither up."

[21] ספתה The plurals of the names of animals are frequently construed with the feminine singular verb regardless of the gender of the nouns, GKC, 154k. In this verse בהמות appears to determine the gender of the verb. The root of the verb is also in question, ספה, as it is taken here, or סוף, "to come to an end."

[22] את-אחריתנו is emended to follow the LXX which reads ὁ θεὸς ὁδοὺς ἡμῶν (ארחותנו). The MT reading captures the same sense but probably results from a metathesis of two letters. See Muilenburg.

12:5

[23] בּוֹטֵחַ has been emended to בּוֹרֵחַ by F. Hitzig, *Der Prophet Jeremia* KHAT (Leipzig: Weidmannsche, 1841) 98; Bernhard Duhm, *Das Buch Jeremia* (Tübingen: J. C. B. Mohr, 1901) 115; Albert Condamin, *Le Livre de Jérémie* (Paris: Librairie Victor Lecoffre, 1920) 102; and to לא בוטח by Walter Baumgartner, *Die Klagegedichte des Jeremia*, BZAW 32 (Giessen: A. Töpelmann, 1917) 52, and Paul Volz, *Der Prophet Jeremia,* KATX (Leipzig: A. Deichert, 1922) 140. A. Ehrman, "A Note on *boteah* in Jer 12:5," *JSS* 5/2 (1960), 153, has argued that no emendation is necessary because the Arabic cognate underlies בוטח meaning "to fall." The same interpretation fits the Targum of Jonathan where the verse is rendered שלמא את-מתבטה ובארעא. Bright, AB, 87, is correct, however, in arguing that what is at stake is Jeremiah's lack of preparation for adversity. If he cannot manage in a safe land, how will he deal with the increasing peril ahead?

12:6

[24] קראו אחרין מלא. The LXX translates καὶ αὐτοὶ ἐβόησαν ἐκ τῶν ὀπίσω σου ἐπισυνήχθησαν (and they have cried out; they are gathered together in pursuit of you). This translation

separates מלא from the verb phrase and explains it. G. R.
Driver, *JSS*, 4-5 (1954), 77-78, proposed that this entire phrase
functioned as a military metaphor for mustering the troops.
Like the Arabic mala'u(n), (full number), it calls Jeremiah's
kinfolk together in pursuit of him. See also J. M. Berridge,
*Prophet, People and Word of Yahweh: An Examination of Form
and Content in the Proclamation of the Prophet Jeremiah*, BST
4 (Zurich: EVZ Verlag, 1970) 98, n. 142.

I. THE PROBLEM OF THE UNITY OF THE CONFESSION

The major critical issue in the interpretation of the first of the "Confessions of Jeremiah" (11:18-12:6) is the problem of the unity of the passage. Three literary observations lead scholars to the conclusion that the
text is in serious dissaray. First, the passage begins abruptly (11:18) leaving מעלליהם without a proper antecedent. The focus of the text is thereby
changed from an indictment of Israel in the preceding lines to a mysterious statement concerning a revelation to the prophet in 11:18. Second,
Yahweh's reply (11:21-23) to Jeremiah's complaint (11:18-20) is ignored in
the rest of the confession (12:1-6). The final verse of the passage (12:6)
suggests that Jeremiah's enemies, identified slightly differently here than
in 11:21-23, have not been subdued as 11:21-23 promise and will continue
to pose a threat to the prophet. Third, the content of v 4, a question about
the duration of the devastation of the land, appears out of joint with the
surrounding verses and, hence, out of context in this confession. These
discordances in the text make it difficult for interpreters to accept it as a
unified poem.

II. PROPOSED SOLUTIONS TO THE PROBLEM
OF THE UNITY OF THE CONFESSION

In an effort to solve the problems related to the unity of the passage,
scholarly treatments rearrange verses, eliminate verses and split the
passage with the purpose of providing a more suitable logical and
chronological arrangement of the passage's content. This chapter begins
with a survey of these scholarly efforts.

A. Rearrangements

1. John Bright[1] relocates 12:1-6 before 11:18-23. This reversal of the verses gives more cohesion to the passage by placing all Jeremiah's complaints before Yahweh's promise of vengeance (vv 21-23). It also provides מעלליהם with a suitable antecedent and removes the abruptness of the opening verse. Jeremiah is now warned before v 18 of the evil deeds of his enemies.

2. More frequently, scholars suggest a simpler rearrangement of the verses. They insert 12:6 between vv 18 and 19 of Chapter 11 to place the warning about the prophet's kinfolk (v 6) before the description of their plots (v 19) and before Yahweh's promise of vengeance (vv 21-23).[2] This alteration seems to give the text more logic because 12:1-5 can now be understood as a development from Jeremiah's personal sufferings (11:18-23) to the broader concern of evil in general.[3]

3. In a similar vein, Rudolph[4] and Weiser[5] transpose verses. Rudolph moves 12:3 after v 20 because v 3 is jarring in its present location, but completes the thought of v 20. Weiser moves 4b in front of 12:3 for the same reasons.

B. Eliminations

1. Because it introduces what appears to be a new subject matter, the duration of the land's devastation, v 4 is the most frequently excised verse

---

[1] AB, 84.

[2] Artur Weiser, *Das Buch des Propheten Jeremiah* I, ATD 20 (Göttingen: Vandenhoeck & Ruprecht, 1952), 105; Sheldon Blank, "The Confessions of Jeremiah and the Meaning of Prayer," HUCA XXI, 339; Wilhelm Rudolph, *Jeremias*, HAT 12 (Tübingen: J. C. B. Mohr, 1968), 89; J. P. Hyatt, "The Book of Jeremiah," *IB* V (Nashville: Abingdon Press, 1956), 912.

[3] H. H. Rowley, "The Text and Interpretation of Jer 11:18-12:6," *AJSLL* XLII (1925/6) 217-227.

[4] Rudolph, *Jeremia*, 89.

[5] Weiser, *Das Buch*, 107.

of the confession. For this reason, some scholars deem it a more suitable fit among the drought materials of c 14.[6]

2. To be consistent, Rowley[7] is forced to discard v 5. He sees it as alien to its present context because he interprets v 5 as a reply to the question of v 4 which he eliminated previously (see above #1).

3. Cornill[8] eliminates v 3a because, in his judgment, its content isolates it from the surrounding materials.

4. Weiser rejects vv 22 and 23 because they are riddled with traditional expressions and, therefore, must be secondary to this confession.[9]

5. Reventlow,[10] McKane,[11] Von Rad[12] and Volz[13] jettison v 6 because, for them, the verse fails to exhibit continuity with v 5.

C. Division of the Passage

Rather than rearrange or eliminate verses of the text, Nicholson[14] and others[15] attempt to solve the problem of the confession's unity by

---

[6]See Rowley, 221; Rudolph, *Jeremia*, 84, who eliminates all but 4Bb; and see also the discussion in Duhm, *Das Buch*, 151.

[7]Rowley, "The Text," 221.

[8]Cornill, *Das Buch Jeremia*, 156.

[9]Weiser, *Das Buch*, 100.

[10]Henning Graf Reventlow, *Liturgie und prophetisches Ich bei Jeremia* (Gütersloh: Gerd Mohn, 1963), 251-257.

[11]W. McKane, "The Interpretation of Jer XII.1-5," *GUOST* (20 (1963-64), 45.

[12]Gerhard Von Rad, "Die Konfessionen Jeremiah," *EvT* 3 (1936), 274.

[13]Paul Volz, *Der Prophet Jeremia*, KAT X (Leipzig: A. Deichert, 1922) 139-142.

[14]E. W. Nicholson, *Preaching to the Exiles: A Study of the Prose Tradition of the Book of Jeremiah* (New York: Schocken Books, 1970).

[15]See Reventlow, *Liturgie*, 240-57; McKane, "The Interpretation," 38-48; Von Rad, "Die Konfessionen," 274; Walter Baumgartner, *Die Klagegedichte des Jeremia*, BZAW 22 (Giessen: A. Töpelmann, 1917), 28-32 and 52-58; Norbert Ittmann, *Die Konfessionen Jeremias: Ihre Bedeutung für die Verkündigung des Propheten*, WMANT 54 (Neukirchen-Vluyn: Neukirchener, 1981), 36-38 and 43.

treating it as two distinct pericopes (11:18-23 and 12:1-6) arising from two separate occasions in the prophet's life.

This brief outline of scholarly treatments reveals that consensus regarding the integrity of the first confession is limited to two conclusions: the text is difficult to interpret because its content appears disorderly and incohesive, and radical surgery is required to restore the text to its original orderly condition. Beyond these agreements, exegetes reach no consensus about what should be transposed or what should be excised. The result is that there are vastly different understandings of the confession's components and widely diverging interpretations of the confession. The following rhetorical and form-critical analyses[16] of 11:18-12:6 argue against these prevailing views to claim that the first confession is a literary unity, if not an original one. The poem presents a cohesive and logical argument regarding Jeremiah's role as a prophet.

III. THE LITERARY STRUCTURE OF JEREMIAH 11:18-12:6

As it presently stands in the MT, this first confession comprises four poetic units (11:18-20; 21-23; 12:1-3; 4-6) which are quite uneven in character. The second unit (vv 21-23) and the last verse of the fourth (v 6) are clearly redactional prose comments, while the first (11:18-20) and the third units (12:1-3) together form a carefully structured poem. The fourth unit (vv 4-6) contains three separate verses loosely connected to the previous units. The purpose of this section is to analyze the interrelationships among these units. The exegesis follows these steps:

(A) It examines the literary connections between the first (11:18-20) and the third (12:1-3) units;

(B) It demonstrates the second unit's redactional nature (11:21-23);

---

[16]Rhetorical-critical analysis is reported before form-critical analysis in the first four chapters of this study, creating the impression that James Muilenburg's essay "Form-Criticism and Beyond," *JBL* LXXXVIII (1969) 1-18, is being disregarded. Muilenburg argues that rhetorical-criticism must build upon form-critical decisions. This study begins with the assumption, disputed seriously by no one since the publication of Baumgartner's *Die Klagegedichte* in 1917, that the confessions are written in the form of the psalm of individual lament. Stylistic decisions proceed from this assumption. However, in several of the confessions, stylistic observations are required before final form-critical decisions can be made.

(C) It discusses the relationship between the fourth unit (vv 4, 5 and 6) and the preceding units.

A. 11:18-20 and 12:1-3

Consideration of the first and third units (11:18-20 and 12:1-3) reveals a symmetry of themes and images, chiastic in nature, that suggests an originally unified poem.

1. 11:18-20

V 18 introduces the first unit with an evocative statement that Yahweh informed Jeremiah (הודיעני) and he became aware of (ואדעה), the deeds of an undefined group of people (מעלליהם). Neither these deeds nor their perpetrators are revealed to the reader in the opening of the poem, a device used to draw the reader further into the poem. In the next verse, through the image of a sheep about to be slaughtered (לטבוח), Jeremiah asserts his innocence of any provocative activity. This innocence includes ignorance (ולא-ידעתי) of the schemes planned against him (מחשבות).

In contrast, a quotation of their conspiratory words reveals the wickedness of Jeremiah's enemies. Depicting him in the image of a tree about to be cut down, the enemies scheme to destroy Jeremiah, to remove his name (ושמו) from memory and to banish him into oblivion. Still, no reason is provided for their hostility toward the prophet. Jeremiah's petition for vengeance (נקמתך אראה) upon his enemeis is expressed in lawsuit language (כי אליך גלית את-ריבי) in v 20. The request is addressed to Yahweh, the Righteous Judge (שפט צדק), Tester of mind and heart (בחן כליות ולב).

2. 12:1-3

Although the third unit employs different language, 12:1-3 moves through some of the same themes and images as 11:18-20 but in reverse order. Moreover, the language and themes of the lawsuit verse (11:20) reappear throughout 12:1-3, further joining the two poems.

In the language of the *rîb* (כי אריב אליך) in v 1, Jeremiah challenges Yahweh, again addressed as a Righteous Judge (צדיק אתה יהוה) with the indicting interrogation, "Why do the wicked flourish?" The very righteousness of Yahweh's judgment is at stake in this attack.

In 2ab, Jeremiah observes that the wicked are like a tree which Yahweh planted (נטעתם), which took root (שרשו), grew (ילכו) and even bore fruit (עשו כרי). Then Jeremiah portrays his enemies as hypocrites with corrupt hearts (מכליותיהם, 2cd).

Contrasting the guilt of his enemies with his own innocence (v 3), the prophet proclaims that Yahweh who knows him (ידעתני), tests his mind (ובחנת לבי) and finds him faithful. Then Jeremiah adds another petition for vengeance in which he requests a reversal of fate. The enemies, not Jeremiah, should become sheep for the slaughter התקם כצאן לטבחה, v 3).

The linguistic and thematic cohesion between these two units of poetry (11:18-20 and 12:1-3) is particularly striking. An inclusio frames them (ויהוה הודיעני ואדעה, 11:18, and יהוה ידעתני, 12:3). In reverse order within this frame, both units contrast Jeremiah's innocence (11:19a; 12:3ab) with the wickedness of the enemies (11:19bcd; 12:2cd). In similar language, both units present the images of a tree to be destroyed (11:19c; 12:2ab) and sheep to be slaughtered (לכבות, 11:19a; לטבחה, 12:3cd). Both use lawsuit terminology (כי אריבי אליך, 11:20; כי אליך גליתי את-ריבי, 12:1) and address Yahweh as Righteous Judge (11:20; 12:3). In both, the Judge engages in similar legal activities (בחן כליות ולב, 11:20; מכלי ותיהם, 12:2). ובחנת לבי, 12:3; Both units close with a petition for vengeance upon the enemies (11:20b; 12:3). Finally, both units make use of these similar themes and images for the same purpose—to invoke Yahweh's vengeance upon Jeremiah's enemies. The chart below illustrates the remarkable affinities between the two poetic pieces.

v 18   Introduction   ויהוה הודיעני ואדעה

    v 19ab   Jeremiah's innocence, a sheep
          for slaughter, is   לכבות

        v 19c   contrasted with the wickedness of the
                 enemies. Jeremiah is a tree to be destroyed.

           v 20   Rîb, Yahweh is Righteous Judge.
                Petition for vengeance
                                        שפט צדק

          v 1   Rîb, Yahweh is Righteous Judge.
                                            צדיק

        v 2   The wickedness of the enemies,
              who are a tree to be destroyed, is
                                     יהוה ידעתני

    v 3   contrasted with Jeremiah's innocence.
        The wicked are sheep for the slaughter.
                                        לטבחה

Petition for vengeance

The prominence of the material from 11:20 in 12:1-3, the thematic symmetry between the two pieces (11:18-20 and 12:1-3) and the presence of the framing device indicate that 11:18-20 and 12:1-3 form a poetic whole. Such may have been the view of the scribe who inserted תראני in 12:3 to extend the frame created by that verse and 11:18. Additional support for this opinion comes from the interruptive and redactional character of vv 21-23.

B. 11:21-23

The prose comment of 11:21-23 separates two strophes of the poem. A number of literary features indicate the redactional character of these verses. They are set off from the surrounding materials by another framing device (על-אנשי ענתות, 21; אל-אנשי ענתות, 23). They play on the word מות which is repeated three times in vv 21-23 to create cohesion among the verses. With the exception of the word שם (vv 19, 21), the verses lack linguistic and stylistic connections with the surrounding materials. Even the one word found in common between the redactional comment and the poem is applied differently in each. In v 19 the enemies attempt to blot out Jeremiah's name; in v 21 they plan to kill him for speaking in Yahweh's name. Furthermore, they interrupt the poetic symmetry described above to function as commentary or midrash upon vv 18-20. This makes explicit the cause of the persecution related in vv 18-20 and promises fulfillment of Jeremiah's request for vengeance. Finally, the language they use to describe the punishment of the men of Anathoth appears inflated and rhetorical in relation to their unexecuted schemes. In the same vein, the language of punishment wrought by sword and famine is generally reserved in the Book of Jeremiah to describe punishment upon the whole people.[17]

Taken together these literary considerations establish the redactional nature of vv 21-23. Their purpose is midrashic, that is, they explain what has been left vague in the opening strophe of the poem (11:18-20). The enemies are identified, their motivation described and their ultimate failure promised. Furthermore, the redactional comment aligns the prophet with Yahweh's cause and aligns the men of Anathoth with the people of

---

[17]Cf., 14:12-15, 18; 15:6; 16; 21:7-9; 27:13; 29:18; 38:2; 42:7, 22; 44:12, 13, 18, 27.

Israel. In v 19 the prophet's name (שם) is to be removed from memory, while in the redactional comment (v 21) he is to be killed for prophesying in Yahweh's name (שם). In effect, the obliteration of the prophet's name also means the obliteration of Yahweh's name from Israel. Similarly, the use of the highly rhetorical language of punishment for the men of Anathoth (v 22) may indicate that they represent all the people who, like them, reject the word of the prophet.

The placement of the prose comment between the two similar poetic strophes highlights Yahweh's promise of vengeance thereby creating a circular movement of thought. The same images appear and reappear in the poem and its editorial comment to form an artistic literary unity.[18] Against the claims of the scholarship discussed earlier, the elimination of verses from the passage or the division of the passage seriously disturbs the present redactional coherence of the poem.

Bright's proposal[19] to reverse pieces of the confessions (11:18-23, and 12:1-6) to solve the problem of the abruptness of v 18 and to provide chronological order to the content, must be discounted on the same grounds. A comparison of this confession with the others indicates that each of them, especially 15:10-21 and 20:7-14, begins mysteriously and dramatically. This literary device leads the reader into the poetry by alluding to events which are revealed later and only partially. An enigmatic opening line appears to be a characteristic feature of the confessions.

C. 12:4-6

The fourth unit (12:4-6) does not cohere quite as neatly with the other materials in the confession, but this chapter claims that these verses fit well in their present contexts. Each verse is treated separately below.

---

[18]See G. R. Castellino, "Observation on the Literary Structure of Some Passages in Jeremiah," *VT*, XXX/4 (1980), 398-408, for other examples of circular literary structure in Jeremiah.

[19]Bright argues that v 18 cannot be the beginning of the piece because it clearly refers back to a divine word received and so requires an antecedent of some kind, AB, 89. Bright fails to compare this confession with the others and so draws the wrong conclusion from a correct observation. That Jeremiah has had a special and mysterious revelation from Yahweh is an essential component of the confessions' argument and does not require an antecedent. See below.

1. Frequently, v 4 is jettisoned from the confession by scholars who judge that its material is alien to the confession and that it fits more readily with the drought material of c 14. The presence of drought imagery, however, provides insufficient warrant for eliminating the verse.

The drought language of 12:4, the land "mourns" (אבל), "dries up" (יבש), or the common synonym, "languishes" (אמלל), appears often in prophetic literature as a motif of judgment upon the people's breach of covenant (Amos 1:2; 8:8; 9:5; Isa 33:9; Joel 1; Jer 4:27-28, 14, 23:10 and Hos 4:3). In these occurrences the drought and devastation of the land arise as the consequence of the people's sin. In Jer 23:10, Jeremiah prophesies that the land will mourn (אבל) and the wilderness will dry up (יבש) because of the curse brought upon it by the false prophet's treachery. In most of the instances listed above, the actual description of a drought is not at issue as it is in Joel 1 and Jer 14. Instead, the issue is the people's disobedience and the disaster which results.

Of particular interest for the discussion of Jer 12:4 is Hos 4:3. This verse forms the closing line of a prophetic judgment speech (4:1-3) which announces Yahweh's lawsuit against Israel. Yahweh is the Judge who indicts the people for covenant infidelities (v 2) and then inflicts the sentence—the total devastation of the land (v 3). In this case, drought is the legal consequence of breach of covenant. The land mourns (תאבל הארץ) and the inhabitants within her languish (ואמלל כל-יושב בה). In Jer 12:4, the land also mourns (תאבל הארץ), and the grass dries up (ייבש) because of the inhabitants within her (ישבי-בה). In both texts the beasts (בהמות, Hos 4:3; בחית השדה, Jer 12:4) and the birds (ובעוף השמים, Hos 4:3; ועוף, Jer 12:4) will be destroyed (יאספו,[20] Hos 4:3; ספתה, Jer 12:4) because of the people's sin (Hos 4:2; Jer 12:4be).

There can be little doubt that Jeremiah is drawing upon the same motifs and traditional language as the Hosea text. But whether originally part of the preceding poetry, or more likely, placed redactionally next to it,[21] the conventional drought material serves a different purpose in Jer 12:4 than it does in the Hosea passage. The legal sentence issued by the Judge in Hos 4:3 is converted in Jer 12:4 into an accusation against the Judge himself. This reversal is accomplished by turning the indictment into a question and by placing it after Jeremiah's first question in 12:1.

The result is that Jer 12:4 now functions as part of Jeremiah's covenant

---

[20]For this meaning of אסף see H. W. Wolff, *Hosea*, Hermeneia, Gary Stansell, trans. (Philadelphia: Fortress Press, 1974), 68.

[21]William L. Holladay, *Architecture*, 134.

lawsuit against Yahweh. It is a second charge against the righteousness of the Righteous Judge. Furthermore the theme of the devastation of the land reappears in the immediately following lament of Yahweh (12:7-13) which indicates that the verse is important to its context and may even have been inserted to help tie Yahweh's lament with the confession. V 4, therefore, should neither be removed from nor displaced in Jeremiah's confession.

2. The enigmatic first verse (v 5) of Yahweh's reply to the prophet (vv 5-6) comprises two parallel questions in the form of mini-parables. Since there is neither linguistic nor stylistic evidence to connect this verse with the earlier pieces of the passage, it is difficult to decide whether v 5 served originally as a response to the preceding poem, or whether it was redactionally juxtaposed with it later. From the perspective of content, the relationship of v 5 to the questions of 12:1-4 is not without difficulty, for the verse directly addresses neither of Jeremiah's questions to Yahweh. Despite this evasion, or more precisely, because of it, the verse fits the pattern of Yahweh's responses to indictments against his justice found elsewhere in the OT.

In the Book of Job, for instance, Yahweh replies to Job's charges that God rules human events unjustly[22] by pointedly changing the subject. Yahweh's failures of justice give way to poetry about the order and design in the universe.[23] Similarly, Yahweh answers Habakkuk's cry of "how long?" (עד-אנה, Hab 1:1-4) with an oracle of terror promising increased chaos and suffering (Hab 1:5). And within another Jeremianic confession (15:10-21), Yahweh ignores the accusation that he behaves like a treacherous wadi (15:18) and shifts the attention to Jeremiah's fidelity (15:19). In each of these cases Yahweh turns the attention from the justice of divine governance to other matters, as if that justice were beyond question.

These comparisons demonstrate that 12:5 fits the pattern of such divine replies seen elsewhere in the OT. Consequently, this verse should remain in its present location. In it Jeremiah is rebuked by the revelation that his dissatisfaction with events is premature for events will surely get worse. The movement of the argument of the verse's two parables is the same, from the lesser to the greater. Both portray an event in which the

---

[22]See the speeches of Job in Jb 1-31.
[23]The same literary characteristics distinguish 11:17 from the oracle upon which it comments, 11:15-16.

discomfort of the present escalates into much greater difficulty in the future. And, like the reply to Jeremiah in c 15, this reply turns away from the questions of theodicy to the matter of the prophet's behavior.

(3) V 6 is appended to v 5 to give concrete substance to the dire predictions about the prophet's future. Evil is accelerating even now. The verse's triple use of גם emphasizes the immediacy and prevalence of the troubles facing Jeremiah. Even his father's house deals treacherously (בגד) with him. Connected to 12:1 by the word בגד and to v 5 by the introductory כי, it seems likely that v 6 is a redactional comment upon v 5.

Several factors lend weight to this suspicion. First, although the difference between prose and poetry is not always clear in the Book of Jeremiah, the style of this verse with its triple גם and its confused meter indicates that it is written in prose form. Second, like 11:21-23, and like 11:17, v 6 makes explicit the enigmatic content of the previous verse. Third, v 6 connects Yahweh's reply (vv 5-6) with the earlier material of the confession, that is, with Jeremiah's enemies alluded to in 11:18-20, 12:1-3 and identified as the men of Anathoth, his own village, in vv 21-23. Fourth, v 6 portrays Jeremiah's enemies, members of his own house, as hypocrites who speak well but act treacherously toward him. Analogously, Yahweh's enemies, the people of his house (12:7ff), are hypocrites who speak well (12:2) but act treacherously בגדי בגד, 12:1). Since the redactor has identified the cause of Jeremiah's persecution by his enemies as his prophetic activity (11:21), it may be that in v 6 he is more strongly identifying the prophet with Yahweh. The enemies of Yahweh and the prophet are the same.

So far this chapter has argued that the first confession comprises a two-strophe poem (11:18-20, 12:1-3) interrupted by a redactional prose comment (11:21-23) and supplemented by three loosely connected verses (12:4-6), the last of which is certainly redactional. If these arguments are correct, rearrangements of the text into separate pericopes are incorrect because they disrupt the literary integrity of the passage as it now stands. The passage, therefore, must be read on two levels, that of the prophet and that of a later editor.[24]

---

[24]At this point in the investigation the identity of the editor cannot be established. The many stylistic differences between the prose of 11:21-23 and the poetry, however, strongly argue against Jeremianic authorship of these verses.

At the level of the original poem, Jeremiah complains that he is wrongly persecuted and asks for vengeance from the Just God. Then he turns this lament around to challenge that Just God and to ask why evil is allowed to continue. Yahweh is charged with planting, nourishing and fostering the growth of the evil ones who are Yahweh's own enemies (12:2), and again Jeremiah demands vengeance upon those enemies.

For the prophet, the confidence that the enemies of Yahweh's word would be punished was a matter of hope. But this theological assumption was called into question by the very circumstances of his life. Thus his *rîb* against Yahweh was utterly appropriate. Jeremiah asks, in light of his own innocent suffering[25] (11:18-20), not only why the wicked prosper and faithless flourish, but why the whole land, Yahweh's land (v 4), is to be destroyed because of these nefarious people.

Yahweh's answer (12:4-6) side-steps the challenge to divine justice and, instead, warns the prophet, without providing any specifics, that the going will get worse. This is all the prophet is told. He is left in the ambiguity of his historical predicament to face the plots against his life and the efforts to blot out even the memory of his name.

At the level of the editorial addition, a redactor sandwiched Yahweh's promise of vengeance between these two pieces of poetry. The framing of this reply by the twin strophes serves to highlight Yahweh's answer and to make it the literary focus of the passage. Yahweh's justice will be done. The word of his prophet will prevail, while those who reject that word, those who attempt to obliterate him from the land, will be vanquished in the year of their punishment.

It is the redactor who informs us that the reason for all this conspiracy and persecution is Jeremiah's prophetic mission (v 21). The theological crisis for the redactor is whether God's word will triumph over history and over the hostility of Yahweh's own people to that word. It is also the redactor who reveals that the members of the prophet's own house rejected his message and acted toward him just as Yahweh's enemies behave toward him, with only vocal loyalty (v 6, v 20). Implicit in the latter revelation is the charge that the people were responsible for the looming catastrophe.

---

[25]Rudolph in *Jeremia*, 84-86, is correct in rejecting the argument that, in 12:1-3, Jeremiah is no longer concerned with his own suffering but has turned to the matter of universal suffering and evil. VV 18-20 provide the incident which leads to the broader question of the triumph of evil.

IV. FORM-CRITICAL ANALYSIS OF
JEREMIAH 11:18-12:6

At first glance, a form-critical analysis of the confession seems to support the opposite view from that taken so far in this chapter. The presence of double complaints suggests that the text should be divided into two separate pericopes (11:18-23; 12:1-6). However, closer investigation reveals that this is not the case. The confession does not contain a pure literary form. Rather it creatively adapts the psalm of individual lament to serve a specific theological purpose.

The ideal form of the psalm of the individual lament includes the following components:

1. Direct address to Yahweh.
2. Complaint or description of the speaker's predicament.
3. Plea of innocence on behalf of the speaker.
4. Statement of trust that Yahweh will intervene.
5. Petition for divine intervention.
6. An oracle of assurance.
7. Vow or expression of praise.[26]

While the psalms of individual lament never become rigidly stereotyped, and hence, few psalms contain all the elements listed above, several of these components are considered constitutive of the form. These are the complaint, the petition for intervention, the confession of trust and the expression of praise.

Jeremiah's confession contains some of these elements.

1. The direct address is found in v 20 and v 3, but not at the opening of the piece as expected.
2. There are two complaint elements, 11:18-19; 12:1-2.
3. The plea of innocence is present in a veiled way in v 18 and more clearly in v 3.
4. There are two petitions for divine intervention, v 20 and v 4.
5. The oracle of assurance is represented by the redactional

---

[26]Artur Weiser, *The Psalms*, OTL, Herbert Hartwell, trans. (Philadelphia: Westminster, 1962), 69: and see Claus Westermann, *The Psalms: Structure, Content and Message* (Minneapolis: Augsburg, 1980), 55-56.

comment, vv 21-23, and by the divine reply, vv 5-6, which
may be loosely designated an oracle of assurance.[27]

Of the constitutive elements of the psalm, two are lacking in the confession, the statement of trust and the expression of praise. These
absences are particularly noteworthy since the purpose of this lament
form is to express praise and confidence in Yahweh in the midst of suffering. However, the two constitutive elements lacking from this confession
are the precise components which would make such a purpose explicit.
Their omission makes the expression of confidence in Yahweh little more
than an implicit intention of the passage. Therefore, it could be said that
Jeremiah plays with the lament form,[28] creatively adapting it to the content of his message. He uses it to express the conflict between his trust
and confidence in Yahweh, on the one hand, and that same God's failure to
act in the predicament of his own life and mission, on the other hand.

The confession ends in paradox. The Righteous God is left unassailable
in his righteousness and the prophet is confronted by a grim future of
increasing gloom. The unidentified redactor assures the audience that
Yahweh will vindicate the prophet and fulfill his word (11:21-23), but he
also relates that the rejection of the word has spread even to the
prophet's house (12:6).

---

[27]It is possible that the duplication of each of these elements
indicates that the confession developed from one psalm of individual
lament after which the second was patterned. Nicholson, for example, in
Jeremiah 1-25, CBC (Cambridge: University Press, 1973), 113-114, argues
that 12:1-6 served as the model for the entirely separate 11:18-23. But
this is unlikely because of the prevalence of the language of 11:20
throughout 12:1-3 which seems to play on the verse itself. There is, however, insufficient evidence to reconstruct the development of the confession. All that can be said firmly is that, in its present state, it forms a
literary unity. Franz D. Hubmann, *Untersuchungen zu den Konfessionen
Jer 11:18-12:6 und 15:10-21*, FB 30 (n.p.: Echter, 1978), 92-93, holds a
similar view.
[28]Even if all of vv 4-6 were redactionally placed, the psalm of
individual lament form is visible in the text because 11:18-20 and 12:1-3
contain the constitutive elements of the complaint and the plea for divine
intervention.

V. THE PURPOSE OF THE CONFESSION

The purpose of the first confession is to establish the legitimacy of Jeremiah's claim to be a true prophet of Yahweh. The strength of this argument, which forms a major thesis of this study, will become clear only when all five of the confessions have been analyzed. The argument can be begun in a preliminary way, however, by considering the elements of this confession which contribute to it.

First, the poem presents Jeremiah as specially connected to Yahweh. Yahweh reveals Jeremiah's dangerous predicament to him (11:18). Yahweh tests Jeremiah and finds him faithful (12:3). Second, the poem claims for Jeremiah innocence of any wrongdoing in the face of bitter persecution by his enemies (11:19). He is in the right, they in the wrong (12:5). Third, the poem blames Yahweh for the prophet's predicament (12:1-2). Fourth, the poem quotes Yahweh's promise that the prophet will meet further rejection (12:5).

It is the last component of the prophet's claim which is most important. The oracle from Yahweh reveals that the circumstances which Jeremiah faces are not unexpected. The true prophet must be prepared to confront even more extraordinary difficulties ahead. His calling should not be placed in question because of his sufferings. Chapter 6 shows that these features of Jeremiah's confession serve to set him apart from the false prophets who plague his ministry and among whom he is classed by his contemporaries. But unlike the false prophets, he is closely identified with Yahweh. He is the innocent one and his suffering is validated by divine oracle.

The theological claims of this confession appear even more clearly in light of the redactional additions, the broader purposes of which must also be established later in this study. The redactional vv 21-23 provide the reason for Jeremiah's persecution. He suffers because he is a prophet. These enemies of his prophecy will not prevail over him for in the end Yahweh will vindicate him. Meanwhile, the opposition to this prophetic word, opposition which is divinely acknowledged (12:6), has accelerated to include his own kinfolk (12:6). One function of these redactional verses, therefore, is to underscore the prophetic claim to authenticity by showing that Yahweh is aware of the persecution of Jeremiah and will vindicate him eventually. The next four confessions develop this argument even more explicitly.

2

The Second Confession:
Jer 15:10–21

TRANSLATION

15:10   Woe is me, my mother, that[1] you bore me,
a man of strife and a man of contention[2] to the whole land.
I did not lend and they did not lend to me,[3]
(yet) all[4] of them curse me.

15:11   So be it,[5] Yahweh, if I have not served you[6] for good,
If I have not entreated you for the enemy[7] in time of trouble
and
in time of distress.

15:12   [8]Can iron break iron[9] from the North[10] and bronze?

15:13   Your strength and your treasures I will give for booty
[11]as the price for all[12] your sins within all[12] your borders.

15:14   I will lead[13] your enemies into a land you do not know
for a fire is kindled in my anger,
against you all it is kindled.

15:15   [14]You know.
Remember me, Yahweh, and visit me.
Take vengeance for me upon my pursuers.[15]
Know I bear reproach on account of you.

15:16   Your words were found and I devoured them.
Your words became a joy to me

and the delight of my heart
because I am called by your name, Yahweh of hosts.[16]

15:17 I have not sat in the circle of merrymakers and made merry.
I have sat alone because of your hand upon me
for you have filled me with indignation.

15:18 Why has my pain become endless
and my wound incurable, refusing to be healed?
You have become to me like a deceitful spring,[17]
waters that are not reliable.

15:19 Therefore, thus says Yahweh,
If you return, I will restore you,
Before me you will stand.
And if you speak what is precious
and not what is worthless,[18]
then you will be as my mouth.
They will turn to you but you will not turn to them.

15:20 And I will make you for this people,
an impregnable wall of bronze
and they will fight you,
but they will not prevail over you
for I am with you to save you and deliver you,
says Yahweh.

15:21 And I will deliver you from the hand of the wicked,
And I will redeem you from the grasp of the violent.[19]

TEXT-CRITICAL NOTES

15:10   [1] כי The LXX reads ὡς τίνα με ἔτεκες (who has borne me),
translating כי י as מי.

[2] מדון Many scholars read ומדון with some MSS and the LXX,
but Muilenburg is correct in pointing out that the prophet is
fond of such pairs.

³The LXX reads this line as οὔτε ὠφέλσα οὔτε ὠφέλησεν με οὐδείς "I have not owed nor has anyone owed me."

⁴ כֻּלֹּה should be כֻּלְהֶם. מְקַלְלוּנִי makes no sense and is emended to קִלְלוּנִי with Rudolph, *Jeremia*, 90 and Muilenburg. This proposal makes sense of both words.

15:11   ⁵ אמל is emended to אמן following the LXX.

⁶ שֵׁרוּתִךְ is read שֵׁרֵתִיךְ from the root שֵׁרֵת, "to serve," in Piel only. See W. Holladay, *A Concise Hebrew and Aramaic Lexicon of the Old Testament* (Grand Rapids: William B. Eerdmans, 1971) 384.

⁷ אֶת-הָאֹיֵב is transposed here from the end of the verse. See Rudolph, *Jeremia*, 104.

15:12-14 ⁸The text is corrupt. Janzen, *Studies*, 133 argues that 15:12-14 are intrusive and related in origin to 17:1-4 (see Bright, AB, 109-110 and Rudolph, *Jeremia*, 104). According to Janzen, these lines may have served originally as a scholarly marginal cross-reference. Their attraction to 15:11 is explained by the possibility that 15:11ff. and 17:1-4 stood in adjacent columns in an ancient manuscript. It is conjectured in this hypothesis that 15:12-14 may have originated as a marginal variant of 17:1-4 or as a correction (since corrupted) of the haplography in the common archetype of 17:1-4, wrongly restored. A. Marx in "A propos des doublets du livre de Jérémie, Reflections sur la formation d'une livre prophétique" in J. A. Emerton, ed., *Prophecy: Essays Presented to Georg Fohrer* (Berlin: Walter de Gruyter, 1980) 106-120, however, has claimed that the doublets in Jeremiah, including this one, are deliberately placed by the redactor to apply words to the whole people which were originally aimed at the prophet or at one segment of the population.

15:12   ⁹ ברזל is lacking in its second occurrence in the LXX, but the Greek text is probably defective by haplography. See Janzen, *Studies*, 117.

¹⁰ מְצֻפוֹן וּנְחֹשֶׁת is translated in the LXX as καὶ περιβόλαιον

χαλκοῦν (and a brass covering), perhaps reading וּמִצְפּוֹן נחשת from צפה (to overlay).

15:13   [11] לא is omitted following the LXX and 17:3. See also L. C. Allen, "More Cockoos in the Textual Nest: At 2 Kings XXIII.5; Jeremiah XVII.3,4: Micah III.3; VI.16 (LXX)," *JTS* 24 (1973) 69-73.

[12] ובכל is read בכל with 17:3 and MSS.

15:14   [13] והעברתי is not emended to follow the LXX and 17:4. See below for a discussion of this decision.

15:15   [14] אתה ידעת is transposed to the end of v 11 by many scholars but there is no good reason to do so.

[15] לְאֶרֶךְ is repointed to לְאָרֶךְ. See Muilenburg.

15:16   [16] אלהי is deleted following the LXX. See Janzen, *Studies*, 81.

15:18   [17] אכזב is a substantized adjective used in place of a noun.

[18]Following the RSV translation.

15:21   [19]Following the JPS translation.

I. THE MAJOR CRITICAL PROBLEM:
THE RELATIONSHIP OF Vv 12-14 TO THE REMAINDER
OF THE CONFESSION

In the long dispute regarding the integrity of the text of this second of the Jeremianic confessions, much of the contention has swirled about the issue of the genuineness of vv 12-14. Critical observations made about these verses cast doubt upon their authenticity. For instance, it is very difficult to decide what v 12 says. Its syntax is unclear, admitting of at least three possible readings.

1. "Is iron broken, iron from the North and bronze?"

2. "Does iron from the North break iron and bronze?"

3. "Can iron break iron from the North and bronze?"[1]

Even when the commentator is able to select one of these possibilities as the best rendering of the line, the difficulties of explaining what the line means in its context and of identifying its speaker still remain.

Moreover, vv 13-14 create a doublet with 17:3-4, themselves an integral part of the larger unit, 17:1-4, but a unit lacking in the LXX. The existence of this doublet, added to the apparent lack of formal and material connection of vv 13-14 with their context, have led many scholars to conclude that these verses have been carried into c 15 through scribal error.

II. PROPOSED SOLUTIONS TO THE PROBLEM OF Vv 12-14

Scholars have solved the problem of the relationship of vv 12-14 with the remainder of the confession in a variety of ways. Some have eliminated one or more of the verses; others have emended various words in the verses; still others have retained the verses but have treated them as secondary, mechanical insertions into the text. Examples of these scholarly treatments of v 12 and vv 13-14 follow.

A. V 12

1. Rudolph, for example, argues tht 15:12 is a corruption of 17:1-2. It was carried into the confession along with 17:3-4 to warn the people concerning their northern enemy. To justify his perception of the verse as a corruption of 17:1-2, Rudolph provides a list of speculative linguistic mutilations scribes may have committed in the transmission of the verse.[2]

2. B. Duhm proposes the following emendation of v 12, suggested to him by the Hebrew text of Jb 6:12. הזרע ברזל באצלי מצהי נחשת ("Is an arm of iron on my shoulders, is my brow bronze?")[3]

---

[1] Condamin, *Le Livre*, 132; K. H. Graf, *Der Prophet Jeremia* (Leipzig: T. O. Weigel, 1862) 225-26; Nicholson, CBC (Cambridge: University Press, 1973), 138.

[2] Rudolph, *Jeremia*, 104.

[3] Duhm, *Das Buch*, 134.

3. Volz, followed by Weiser, also emends the text to solve the problems of syntax and meaning of v 12. He proposes הרעתי ברזל ונחשת and understands Jeremiah as the speaker.[4]

4. Finally, Bright, Cornill and Condamin pursue even more drastic measures, eliminating the verse altogether.[5]

B. Vv 13-14

Although vv 13-14 raise more problems than v 12, there has been far more agreement among commentators about how to deal with them. There are basically two positions. Some scholars, notably Hyatt and Nägelsbach, retain vv 13-14 but judge them as a mechanical insertion without significance for the confession.[6] But by far the majority opinion holds that they should be excised completely from the text because they appear to lack sufficient connection with the surrounding material.[7]

Most of the scholars who remove vv 13-14 then proceed to treat the remainder of the confession (15:10-11, 12, 15-21) as a single literary unit. However, having removed vv 12-14, Baumgartner, Berridge and Lundblom understand the text to contain two distinct, unrelated literary units.[8]

None of the above treatments of v 12 and vv 13-14 is completely satisfactory. These approaches either emend the text extensively to produce only slightly less obscure verses than the MT, or perform radical surgery

---

[4]Volz, Der Prophet, 172; Weiser, Das Buch, 138, n.

[5]Bright, AB, 109-110; and "A Prophet's Lament and Its Answer," Int 28 (1974) 59-74; Cornill, Das Buch, 195-96; Condamin, Le Livre, 131-132.

[6]Hyatt, IB, 941; W. E. Nägelsbach, "The Prophet Jeremiah," in Lange's Commentary on Holy Scripture, VI (Grand Rapids: Zondervan, 1960) 155; see also the proposal in Janzen, Studies, 133, which is discussed briefly above under text-critical notes.

[7]Rudolph, Jeremia, 96; Graf, Der Prophet, 225; Friedrich Giesebrecht, Das Buch Jeremia, HAT (Göttingen: Vandenhoeck & Ruprecht, 1894) 89; Bright, AB, 109-110; Volz, Der prophet, 171; Duhm, Das Buch, 135; Nicholson, CBC, 138; and H. W. Jüngling, "Ich Mache dich zu einer ehernen Mauer: Literarkritische Überlegungen zum Verhältnis von Jer 1:18-19 zu Jer 15:20-21," Bib 54 (1973) 17.

[8]Baumgartner, Die Klagegedichte, 33-40; John Maclennan Berridge, Prophet, People and the Word of Yahweh: An Examination of Form and Content in the Proclamation of the Prophet Jeremiah, BST 4 (Zurich: EVZ, 1970) 114; Jack R. Lundblom, Jeremiah: A Study in Ancient Hebrew Rhetoric, SBLDS 18 (Missoula: Scholars Press, 1975), 28.

to eliminate rather than solve the problems. This chapter offers an alternative view of the relationship of v 12 and vv 13-14 to the rest of the confession. Rooting its argument in an interpretation of the content and context of vv 12-14, it proposes their retention basically as they stand in the MT (however, see text-critical notes above). After the discussion of the critical problem of the passage, a consideration of the integrity of the entire confession, an investigation of its form-critical components and an interpretation of the meaning and purpose of the passage follow.

III. THE RELATIONSHIP OF Vv 12-14 TO THE REMAINDER OF THE CONFESSION

Although vv 12-14 present throny problems to the interpreter, good sense can be made of them in their context. Together these verses function as Yahweh's answer to Jeremiah's complaint in vv 10-11; v 12 conveys a message of assurance to the prophet, while vv 13-14 bring a word of judgment upon the people and promise the vindication of the prophet. The latter two verses have been editorially inserted for the purpose of explaining the implications of vv 11-12. To establish the suitability of retaining these three verses within the confession, it is first necessary to examine them in the context of Jeremiah's complaint (vv 10-11).

A. Vv 10-11

In the opening verse of this confession, Jeremiah's wail to his mother for bringing him to birth receives its specific content from the hendiadys which the prophet uses to describe himself, "a man of strife and a man of contention to the whole land." Jeremiah resents his birth, not for its own sake, but on account of the conflict which characterizes his life. Continually during his life he had been placed in the role of judge of his people. In this verse, as in the cursing poem of 20:14-18 (see Chapter 5), the diversion of attention from the birth motif to Jeremiah's difficult life indicates that the real issue is not his birth but his life, specifically, his prophetic life. The birth motif functions symbolically to connect this complaint (and 20:14-18; see Chapter 7) with the call account in chapter 1 where Jeremiah was appointed a prophet even before his birth (1:5). The whole purpose of Jeremiah's birth, indeed, the reason he went forth from the womb (מרחם תצא) was to be a "prophet to the nations" (1:5). Jeremiah's second confession, therefore, begins with a complaint about his prophetic vocation.

The remaining lines of v 10 add substance to the prophet's lament. Jeremiah is cursed by everyone (10d), although he is innocent of any offense (10c,d). Unfortunately, neither the identification of the prophet's enemies (10d), nor the precise meaning of his refusal to engage in lending practices (10c) is clear. His enemies are probably all the people of the land who resist his message, an interpretation suggested by the juxtaposition of כלהב קללוני (10d, see text-critical note) with לכל-הארץ (10b). His refusal either to lend or to borrow may mean that he literally refrained from engaging in these monetary activities, or if it is a proverbial wisdom saying, it may express Jeremiah's innocence in general.[9]

To this assertion of innocence, v 11 adds a testimony to Jeremiah's fine performance as a prophet. He served Yahweh for good (11a) and he interceded on behalf of the enemy in the time of sorrow and distress (11b,c). The last two lines of v 11 require further comment. First, the enemies mentioned in 10c (see text-critical note) are probably the prophet's own enemies. These are the people who reject his message, an interpretation again suggested by the juxtaposition of remarks about enemies (11c, 10cd). Second, the expression "in time of trouble and in time of distress" (בעת-רעה ובעת צרה), incorporates language (רעה, צרה) used elsewhere in the Book to refer to Yahweh's judgment upon the people.[10] The language of these verses, therefore portrays Jeremiah as a faithful prophet who intercedes for his people on the day of judgment. Jeremiah's fidelity (v 11) and his innocence (10c), contrast strongly with the perverse treatment he receives from his enemies (10d) because of his prophetic calling (10ab). This predicament supplies the context for Yahweh's reply to the prophet in v 12 and for the editorial insertion of vv 13-14.

B. V 12

Employing veiled images which connote rather than denote a solution to the prophet's plight, Yahweh's reply to Jeremiah is cryptic and riddle-like (12:5) in the style of the response in the first confession (11:18-12:6). (See Chapter 1.) Despite the three possible syntactical constructions of 15:12 proposed by Condamin (see above), the verse is best read following its

---

[9]J. D. Michaelis, *Observationes Philologicae et Criticae in Jeremiae Vaticinia et Threnos* (Göttingen: Vandenhoeck & Ruprecht, 1792) 130; Rudolph, *Jeremia*, 107.

[10]For רעה see 5:12; 6:6, 19; 11:11, 17; 17:18; 18:11; 19:3; 20:12; 45:5. For צרה see 14:8; 16:19; 30:7.

most obvious syntactic order, that is, taking the first ברזל as the subject and the second as the object.[11] "Can iron break iron from the North and bronze?"

A similar line in Prov 27:17 may provide a clue to the origin of this oblique verse. "Iron sharpens iron . . ." (ברזל בברזל יחד). The proverb's Hebrew construction is different from Jer 15:12, with the verb coming third and the subject and the object distinguished by the preposition ב.[12] Still, the placement of the two ברזל words next to each other, plus the similarity in content between the verses, make it likely that 15:12 was originally either a proverb or an embellishment of a popular saying. "Can iron break iron" (and bronze?)[13] or "Can iron break iron from the North?" suggest themselves as possible original wordings. Iron from the North may have referred to the "superior" iron of Chalybes mentioned in Virgil's I Georg v 58[14] as particularly strong iron in the estimate of the ancients. Or it may have meant simply the region from which iron came to Palestine.[15]

But whatever one may propose as the components of the hypothetical original, in the confession, this verse is Hebrew poetry. Hence, one can presume that its images were selected as much for their ranges of meaning as for their precise denotations. Within the Jeremianic corpus, צפון and נחשת bear important nuances. In a few instances, צפון refers to the Northern Tribes of Israel invited to reunite with Judah on Zion (3:12, 18). In a few other cases, צפון is the direction from which Israel will return from captivity (23:8; 31:8). But, in most of its occurrences, the North is the direction from which the enemy will come to carry out God's judgment upon Israel (1:14; 4:6; 6:1, 22; 10:22; 13:20; 25:9), upon Babylon (50:3, 9, 41), upon Egypt (46:6, 10, 20, 24) and upon the Philistines (47:2). Among these, several versions depict this enemy from the North metaphorically:

> 1:14 a boiling pot facing the North
> 10:22 a great commotion from the North

---

[11] Reventlow, *Liturgie,* following Raschi, 214, n. 72; and Hyatt, *IB,* 940.

[12] Michaelis reports that Codex Regiom 2 reads ברזל בברל for Jer 15:12, *Observationes,* 135.

[13] Iron and bronze are often paired in the OT texts although frequently in reverse order. Cf., Gen 4:22; Jos 6:9; Num 31:22; 1 Chron 22:4, 16; 29:2; Jer 6:29.

[14] Cited by Michaelis, *Observationes,* 136.

[15] F. W. Winnett, "Iron," *IDB,* II, 725.

46:10 a sacrifice in the North
46:20 a gadfly from the North
47:2 water rising from the North[16]

"Iron from the North" belongs with this list of metaphoric descriptions of the enemy. Although "iron from the North" may denote a strong metal impervious to blows from ordinary iron, it also connotes Israel's foreign enemy.

Though נחשת appears infrequently in the Book of Jeremiah, in its few occurrences, it, too, carries nuances important for the interpretation of 15:12. In the call account, Yahweh assures Jeremiah that he will make him a bronze wall (ולחמת נחשת, 1:18), a promise reiterated in the latter part of this confession (לחומת נחשת, 15:20). In both instances, bronze symbolizes the God-given strength of the prophet in the face of an unbelieving people. The context of the word in 15:12 gives rise to the same conclusion. The prophet's complaint that he is cursed by his enemies in 15:10 and the divine promise that Jeremiah will be made into a bronze wall in v 20 indicate that, in 15:12, bronze is a symbol of the prophet made strong by Yahweh.

If it is correct that "iron from the North and bronze" refer to the foe from the north and the prophet, that is, Yahweh's instruments in the execution of his judgment against Israel, it is probable that the first ברזל represents Israel itself. A consideration of Jer 6:28 adds strength to the case. In that verse, the people are described as נחשת וברזל, a metaphor for their stubborn rebelliousness, and the prophet is depicted as the assayer and tester of ores (6:27).[17]

Yahweh's reply to Jeremiah's complaint, then, provides a word of encouragement to the prophet. "Can iron break iron from the North and bronze?" means "Can Jeremiah's enemies, who appear as strong as iron, break God's instruments, the enemy from the North and the prophet?" At the literal level of the metallic clash and at the symbolic level of the clash of Israel and God's agents, the expected answer is clearly no. Therefore, v 12 belongs in its present location within the confession.

---

[16] See Reventlow, *Liturgie,* 215.

[17] The text of 6:28 is in question (see BHS). However this phrase has been retained by JPS and RSV. But see Bright, AB, 49, n. 27 and Rudolph, *Jeremia,* 48, who delete it on the speculation that it was drawn from 1:18. Its existence in other Jeremianic passages and in Ezek 22:18, 20, however, hardly warrant its deletion here.

C. Vv 13-14

To this reply of Yahweh is added the editorial insertion of vv 13-14. The grounds for deciding that these verses are editorial are the following:

1. Vv 13-14 do not quite fit into the context of the confessions, addressing first the people (v 13) and then the prophet (v 14, but see below).

2. Vv 13-14 function like the redactional additions to the earlier confession (11:21-23; 12:6), to explain and expand the immediately preceding verses (see below).

3. Vv 13-14 promise vengeance upon the prophet's enemies, but v 15 ignores that promise and petitions Yahweh for vengeance. In 14cd, Yahweh's anger bursts forth uncontrollably, but in v 15 Jeremiah is impatient with Yahweh's slowness to anger.

Although the secondary status of these verses is undeniable, it is more difficult to decide which is the original location of these verses, 15:13-14 or 17:3-4. On the one hand, 17:3-4 appears to be an expansion of 15:13-14, adding כל to אוצרותיך in 17:3a and אשר נתתי לך מנחלתך ובך ושמיתה, 14a. 15:13-14 adds only לא and ובכל (13b) and differs from 17:3-4 at only two points: 15:14a reads והעברתי for והעבדתיך of 17:4b and 15:14d reads עליכם for עד-עולם of 17:4d. Moreover, the assumption that 15:13-14 has been inserted and expanded in c 17 might explain the omission of 17:1-4 from the LXX.

On the other hand, 17:3-4 fits quite well as the climax of the accusation in 17:1-2. Although it is possible that vv 1 and 2 were written as a secondary introduction to vv 3 and 4, the editorial pattern observed in the Book so far indicates that expansions tend to be located after the material they are intended to clarify rather than before.[18] Consequently, this paper accepts the majority opinion[19] that 17:3-4 is the original location of these verses.

Having made the decision that 17:3-4 is the prior text, many commentators emend 15:13-14 to accord more completely with that text, and, then, simply treat 15:13-14 as alien material accidentally joined to the

---

[18]11:17 after 15-16; 11:21-23 after 11:20 and 12:6 after 12:5.

[19]Reventlow, *Liturgie*, 212, appears to be the sole dissenter.

confession. However, a plausible argument can be made for the deliberate, although imperfect, adaptation of these verses to their new setting in the confession. Elsewhere in the Book of Jeremiah doublets have been so adapted.[20] Moreover, sense can be made out of the text as it now stands.

The heart of the problem lies in the singular endings of the compound subjects of v 13 (חילך ואוצרותיך). These words make no sense when applied to Jeremiah. In 17:3 they are addressed to the people, and they remain so directed here in the confession. This verse was imported into this context to elaborate the theme of Yahweh's judgment against the people introduced in 11bc. Israel's might and her treasures will become booty in punishment for her sins in the land (15:13).

V 14 continues this expansion of the judgment theme. Not only will Israel become enfeebled and lose possessions, it will also be exiled to an unknown land. The change in verse from והעבדתיך (17:4) to והעברתי, lacking the second singular suffix, also changes the addressee of the line from the people to Jeremiah. "I will lead your enemies into a land you do not know." This verse now performs the additional function of promising vindication to the prophet. When Jeremiah's enemies are carted off into exile, it will become clear that his prophetic word has been reliable. It is helpful to recall here that the editorial comment, 11:21-23, functions to vindicate the prophet's message also (see Chapter 1). If the editor is exilic (see Chapter 9), this verse might also serve to explain v 12 more concretely. Yahweh had, indeed, made his prophet a wall of bronze whose word was fulfilled through the captor, Babylon.[21]

---

[20]For example, see Chapter 5 on 11:20 and 20:12 and see Alfred Marx, "A propos des doublets du livre de Jérémie: Reflexions sur la formation d'un livre prophétique," in *Prophecy: Essays Presented to Georg Fohrer*, ed by J. A. Emerton (Berlin: Walter de Gruyter, 1980) 106-120; and Hubmann's "Exkurs die Doppelüberlieferungen im Jer-buch," *Untersuchungen,* 217-244.

[21]Gerstenberger, "Jeremiah's Complaints: Observations on Jer 15:10-21," *JBL* 82 (1963) 393-408, also retains these verses and reads v 14 with the MT. Of greater importance for this discussion, he understands vv 13-14 to be an editorially inserted oracle of promise. The basis for his view is the significance Gerstenberger ascribes to the omissions in 15:13-14 from 17:3-4. The omissions include the indictment of Israel and the remark that the people "will let go their heritage." After extensive emendations (see n. 12, 395), he interprets v 13 as Yahweh's statement that Israel had atoned for her sins, and v 14, that Babylon will now be led into captivity. The major objection to this view is the absence of other examples of the theme of captivity as atonement within the Book of Jeremiah. Moreover,

Though the above interpretation of vv 13-14 can be held only tentatively, this position has the advantage of providing plausible reasons for
their insertion into the confession. Furthermore, the view gains support
from the recognition that vv 13-14 function in a manner similar to the
previously observed redactional additions to Jeremiah's first confession
(see remarks above on 11:21-23 and 12:6).

IV. THE INTEGRITY OF THE CONFESSION

Attention must now be directed to an investigation of the integrity of
the entire confession. Literary features of formal structure, style and
connections of content indicate that, in its present shape, this confession
forms a coherent literary piece. In this discussion vv 13-14 will be left
aside since they have already been exposed as a secondary addition to the
text. For the purposes of clarity, the text is divided into three units:
(I) vv 10-12, 15; (II) vv 16-18; (III) vv 19-21.[22]

In each of the first two portions of the confession ([I] vv 10-12, 15 and
[II] vv 16-18) the material is arranged in a similar formal structure
expressing Jeremiah's predicament by means of antitheses. In v 10
Jeremiah laments the fact that he was ever born to his prophetic life, yet
in v 15 he begs not to lose that life as a consequence of Yahweh's excessive patience with the enemy. In v 16 the prophet proclaims the joy he
found in Yahweh's words, yet in v 18 he accuses Yahweh of becoming
unreliable, the cause of his unending pain. These first two portions of the
poem also exhibit a relationship of content. The prophet's cry of v 15.
"Know I bear reproach on account of you" becomes the major theme of
vv 16-18.[23]

Although lacking in formal parallels with the preceding two units of the
confession, the third unit (vv 19-21) is connected to them by its content.

---

there still remains the problem of explaining the attraction of this insertion to this passage when there are many other places where the Exile is
more clearly promised than in 15:12.

[22]See below for a form-critical description of the passage.

[23]See Jüngling, "Ich Mache," 160-163. It is also possible that v 15d and
v 18cd provide parallel endings to their units, each making an accusation
against Yahweh. V 15 is ambiguous, however, admitting also of the interpretation that Jeremiah is expressing his own fidelity to Yahweh despite
the reproach that brings upon him. עליך can mean "on account of you" or
"against you."

This portion of the poem contains Yahweh's reply to the two dilemmas or antitheses expressed by the prophet in the previous two units. In the first unit (vv 10-12, 15) Jeremiah laments his innocent suffering and asserts his fidelity as a prophet. In the second unit the prophet complains about the isolation and pain brought upon him by his prophetic vocation even though, again, he claims to have performed all that Yahweh asked of him.

The divine response (vv 19-21) addresses both these complaints. V 20, a doublet of 1:18, assures Jeremiah that, by God's empowerment (20ab) and presence (20c), Jeremiah's enemies will lose their fight against him (20cd). This consoling promise is further emphasized by v 21, which may be a secondary expansion. The editorial nature of this verse is suggested by the presence of נאם-יהוה at the end of v 20, forming a natural conclusion to Yahweh's reply. V 21, moreover, adds no new content to the poem. Instead, it emphasizes Yahweh's saving activity, repeating the verb נצל and adding references to the enemies from whom the prophet is to be saved (מיד רעים, מכף ערצים). The editorial nature of this verse, however, is not certain. The נאם-יהוה may have been Jeremiah's device to emphasize Yahweh's deliverance.

Moreover, Jeremiah's complaints regarding his prophetic office are addressed less directly by this response but they are addressed. The prophet is given conditions by which he will be restored to his prophetic status as Yahweh's mouth and mediator for his people (v 19). And he is assured that he will be given strength in that role (vv 20-21). Although in this confession Jeremiah claims to have performed his tasks faithfully, Yahweh responds to his complaint by insisting that certain conditions must be met for Jeremiah to function as a true prophet. Vv 19-21, therefore, develop themes raised by the first two units of the confession. They are integral to the passage.

In addition to the formal interconnectedness of the first two units and the material relationships among all three units, a stylistic pattern of word repetition with verses also joins the three.

(10b); איש ריב ואיש מדון	(10c); לא-נשיתי ולא נשו-בי	
(11ab); אם-לא אב-לוא	(11c); בעת-רעה ובעת צרה	
(12) ברזל בברזל	(15ac).[24] ידעת דע	
(16ab); דבריך דבריך	(17ab); ישבתי ישבתי	

---

[24]It is difficult to determine if ידעת is a scribal gloss or an original part of the verse. The text is unsettled.

תשוב   ואשיבך (19b);   אם-   ואם- (19b,d);
תשוב אליהם   ישבו . . . אליך (19g).

This analysis of the three units reveals that this confession forms a coherent literary unity. Scholarly interpretations which eliminate verses or divide the passage into two unrelated pericopes have failed to grasp the literary nature of the poem.

V. FORM-CRITICAL DESCRIPTION OF THE CONFESSION

This confession, like the previous one (11:18-12:6), also creatively adapts the form of the psalm of individual lament to express the theological dilemma of the prophet. Its form-critical components can be described as follows:[25]

1. Direct address vv 11a, 15a
2. Complaint vv 10-11, 16-18
3. Plea of Innocence vv 10cd-11, 16-17. (In this confession the pleas of innocence and the complaints merge into one another.)
4. Petition for divine intervention v 15
5. Oracle of assurance vv 12-14, 19-21 (of these, vv 13-14 and possibly v 21 have been identified as editorial expansions).

Of the constitutive elements of the psalm of individual lament form, two are present in this confession, the complaint and the petition. Two are lacking, the statement of confidence and the vow of praise. Since the two missing elements again comprise the formal components which make the purpose of the form explicit—to praise God with confident trust in the midst of adversity—their omission from this second confession also appears theologically significant. That the prophet would use this literary genre at all suggests that he possesses an underlying trust that Yahweh is with him and will vindicate him.

At the same time, the absence of two constitutive features of the form serves to underscore Jeremiah's dilemma. The God whom he wishes to trust has become untrustworthy. Where is the God for whom the prophet delivers words of strife and contention? Where is the God whose power

---

[25]See the discussion of 11:18-12:6 in Chapter 1 for a listing of the components of the ideal form

forces him to sit alone and causes him unceasing pain? Jeremiah's adaptation of the individual lament form expresses the theological predicament
of the prophet waiting for the fulfillment of God's word. Yet this second
confession brings a theological advance over the first one. Here the oracle
of assurance actually offers some hope to the prophet. Although the
prophet himself does not express confidence explicitly, he is promised
restoration as prophetic mediator, and he is promised deliverance from his
enemies.

VI. THE PURPOSE OF THE CONFESSION

The purpose of this confession is to provide credentials of legitimation
for Jeremiah's prophecy. It makes clear that he is a true prophet called by
Yahweh to deliver the word. The argument of the poem develops from the
first verse where the problem is introduced. It reaches its climax and
solution in Yahweh's final reply to the prophet's complaints. There are two
major issues raised by the poem: Jeremiah's relationship to his prophetic
calling and Yahweh's relationship to his prophet.

Jeremiah is at pains to establish his innocence and to proclaim his fidelity to his role as prophet. He served Yahweh for good and interceded for
the enemy in time of judgment (v 11). He devoured Yahweh's word, uniting
himself with the message he was to deliver. He spoke words that were not
his but Yahweh's (v 16ab), a claim emphasized by the repetition of דבריך.
These words became his chief delight (v 16bc) because (כי) he belongs to
Yahweh and was called by Yahweh's name (v 16d).[26] His loyalty to
Yahweh cost him the company of others. He did not sit (ישבתי) with
merrymakers; he sat alone (ישבתי), not because he chose to do so, but
because of Yahweh's power over him (מפני ידך, v 17).

Jeremiah had been truly faithful to his vocation, and so he makes
Yahweh the originator of his difficulties. Yahweh (כי זעם מלאתני) filled
the prophet with indignation (v 17). The one who required so much of his
faithful prophet and who is supposed to be a fountain of living water, has
become a treacherous and deceitful wadi (v 18c). All this complaining and

---

[26]See Carroll, *From Chaos to Covenant: Prophecy in the Book of Jeremiah* (New York: Crossroad, 1981) 223, who perceives this interiorization
of the word as a form of escape into the prophet's inner life. Such psy-
chologizing of the confessional text totally distorts its purpose.

accusation serves to establish Jeremiah's case that he is the loyal prophet who has performed all his activities under the aegis of Yahweh.

The divine response to the prophet's complaints certifies Jeremiah's claims that his calling is genuine and that Yahweh is indeed with him. The messenger formula which opens the response (לכן כה אמר יהוה, v 19a) has been viewed by Gerstenberger as evidence that vv 19-21 comprise late Deuteronomistic material. This is because he judges that the private nature of the oracle deprives the formula of anything but an emphatic function.[27] But by reducing the confession to no more than a private oracle,[28] Gerstenberger misses the purpose of the confession—to legitimate Jeremiah over against the false claimants to the prophetic office. The messenger formula serves its usual purpose here. It makes clear that the oracle to follow is Yahweh's word and that its speaker, Jeremiah, has been authorized to pronounce it.

This oracular response is puzzling. It begins with a rebuke of the prophet after he has just established his loyalty to his calling. Though context may suggest that the rebuke is a response to Jeremiah's audacious accusations against Yahweh (v 18), it seems more likely that the oracle is intended to assure the audience that there are conditions to be met before one is able to claim to be a true prophet. The prophet must turn toward Yahweh (v 19b) and must speak what is true and not what is worthless (v 19b). When these conditions are met the prophet will stand before Yahweh and will be Yahweh's mouth. Undoubtedly, standing before Yahweh means that the prophet will be admitted to the heavenly council (Jer 18:23; 1 K 22:19ff.) to hear Yahweh's word and to serve as mediator and intercessor (Jer 15:1). When these conditions are met, the prophet will be recognized as the true mediator, but he will not serve the faithless people in that capacity (v 19g).

Throughout this oracular response to Jeremiah's predicament, emphasis has been placed upon the action and power of Yahweh. He will restore the prophet (v 19b); he will make the prophet an impregnable wall; he will save and redeem the prophet (vv 20-21). In the complaints of this

---

[27] Gerstenberger, "Jeremiah's Complaints," supports his thesis with a discussion of what he terms the abstract theological language of the passage said to be typical of the Deuteronomists. In addition to misunderstanding the purpose of the passage, Gerstenberger also fails to consider the continuity of thought among the levels of tradition in the book (see Chapter 1) and, the accompanying difficulty of distinguishing levels on the basis of theological motifs alone.

[28] See Bright, AB, 111.

confession, Jeremiah claimed for himself the office of true prophet and this oracle places upon him the seal of approval, a public seal. He is the prophet like Moses into whose mouth Yahweh has set his word (Dt 18:18).

3

The Third Confession:
Jer 17:14–18

TRANSLATION

17:12   A throne of glory on high from the beginning is the place of our
        sanctuary.[1]

17:13   Hope of Israel, Yahweh,
        all who have forsake you will be ashamed;
        those who turn aside[2] will be written in the earth
        for they have forsaken the spring of living waters, Yahweh.

17:14   Heal me, Yahweh, and I will be healed.
        Save me and I will be saved,
        for you are my praise.[3]

17:15   They are now saying to me,
        "Where is the word of Yahweh?
        Let it come "

17:16   I have not pressed you for evil[4]
        I have not longed for the calamitous day[5]
        You know the utterances of my mouth.
        They were ever before you.[6]

17:17   Do not be a terror to me.
        You are my refuge in the day of distress.

17:18   Let my pursuers be shamed
        and do not let me be shamed.
        Let them be terrified

but do not let me be terrified.
Bring upon them the evil day
and shatter them with double destruction.

TEXT-CRITICAL NOTES

17:12   [1] מראשון מקום is lacking in the LXX due to haplography. See
Janzen, *Studies*, 117. Muilenburg suggests the following tricola
of vocatives for this verse: "O throne of glory . . . , O place of
our sanctuary, O Hope of Israel."

17:13   [2] יְטוּרַי is corrected to וְסוּרֶיהָ with Rudolph, *Jeremia*, 116.

17:14   [3] תְּהָתָּי is emended to תְּחַלְּהִי by Volz, *Der Prophet*, 186, which
suits the context well.

17:16   [4] מֶרְעֶה is corrected fo לְרָעָה following Muilenburg and Rudolph,
Jeremia, 116

           [5] אָנוּשׁ is translated in the LXX as ἀνθρώπου (אֱנוֹשׁ) but אָנֻשׁ
fits the context better.

[6]Following the JPS.

I. THE CRITICAL PROBLEM:
Vv 12-13

The one serious critical issue in the interpretation of the third and
briefest of the Jeremianic confessions is the problem of the relationship
of vv 14-18 to vv 12-13. On the one hand, the verses seem intrusive
because the context of vv 12-13 does not fit easily with the body of the
confession (vv 14-18) nor with the wisdom saying in v 11. On the other
hand, vv 12-13 exhibit stylistic and linguistic connections with vv 14-18.
Linguistically, the repetition of יבשׁו joins vv 13 and 18. Stylistically, the
repetition of עזב within v 13 represents a typical pattern of repeated

words found in the other confessions[1] and, in another form, in vv 14 and 18 of this confession. (See below.)

A small number of scholars who place greater weight upon the connections among these verses than upon their differences judge that vv 12-13 form an integral part of the confession. For example, Condamin includes vv 12-13 in the confession because words are repeated within it and because symmetry is created by groups of verses throughout it.[2] Baumgartner,[3] followed by Berridge,[4] has proposed a form-critical argument for the same delimitation of the passage. They argue that vv 12-13 serve as a hymnic introduction to the confession. Although Old Testament parallels for such a form-critical structure are few and late,[5] Baumgartner finds supporting parallels among Babylonian and Assyrian laments. These commonly begin with hymnic introductions.[6] Weiser develops Baumgartner's form-critical argument further by claiming that this hymnic prelude portrays a theophanic cultic experience similar to that found in Isaiah's call narrative.[7]

The majority of scholars, however, place more emphasis upon the dissonance between the two sets of verses than upon their harmony. They understand vv 12-13 either as a secondary gloss or as a distinct literary unit and eliminate them from the confession.[8] Although some commentators have discarded vv 12-13 solely on the dubious theological

---

[1]See Chapter 2.

[2]Condamin, *Le Livre*, 147; see also Norbert Ittmann, *Die Konfessionen Jeremias: Ihre Bedeutung für die Verkündigung des Propheten*, WMANT 54 (Neukirchen-Vluyn: Neukirchener, 1981) 49.

[3]Baumgartner, *Die Klagegedichte*, 40-44.

[4]Berridge, *Prophet*, 137-151. See Reventlow, *Liturgie*, 228 and Carroll, *From Chaos*, 121-123, both of whom find a cultic hymn in the text.

[5]Ps 80:2; Neh 15:5, 9:6; Dan 9:4.

[6]Baumgartner, *Die Klagegedichte*, 40-41.

[7]Weiser, *Das Buch*, 152-153. Lundblom, *Jeremiah*, 88-89, alone proposes that the kernel of the confession includes vv 13-16a, which, he asserts, has been expanded by the later addition of 16b-18. The basis for this assignment of verses to the confession is his discovery of a chiasmus of speakers in the proposed original kernel. His use of this criterion, however, requires the elimination of large portions of the verses without the support of other literary warrants.

[8]Duhm, *Das Buch*, 147; Sigmund Mowinckel, *Zur Komposition des Buches Jeremiah*, Videenskapsselskapets Skrifter 11 (Kristiania, 1914) 20, n. 3; Bright, AB 119; Cornill, *Das Buch*, 216; Rudolph, *Jeremia*, 117; Thiel, *Redaktion*, 203; Nicholson, CBC, 150; and even Thompson, *The Book*, 425.

grounds that they contradict the message of Jeremiah's temple sermon,[9] there are strong arguments for limiting the confession to vv 14-18.

Vv 14-18 are composed of short, balanced clauses of nearly equal length, while vv 12-13 consist of longer, less-balanced clauses that do not blend rhythmically with those of the confession. Furthermore, two literary features of the confession show that vv 14-18 form a discrete literary unity. These verses are framed by parallel clauses (vv 14 and 18) in which words are repeated in nearly identical fashion.

14a	רפאני יהוה וארפא
14b	הושיעני ואושעה
18a	יבשו רדפי ואל-אבשה אני
18b	יחתו המה ואל-אחתה אני

Throughout these verses personal pronouns are employed in a striking manner to distinguish further vv 14-18 from vv 12-13.

אתה (14c);	המה (15a);	ואני (16a);
אתה (17b);	אני (18a);	המה (18b);
אתה (16c);		
אני (18b).		

Moreover, the abstract, impersonal tone of adoration of vv 12-13 appears more appropriate to a communal hymn than to the confessions. The latter are characterized by personal complaint and by concrete depictions of Yahweh.[10] Finally, hymnic introductions are lacking from all the other confessions. Each confession opens abruptly and personally as does v 14.

Without vv 12-13, vv 14-18 form a balanced literary unit, while the inclusion of vv 12-13 can be supported neither form-critically nor materially. Moreover, liturgical passages such as vv 12-13 appear elsewhere and also stand as independent pieces (14:7-9; 14:19-21; 16:19-20). Vv 12-13 should be eliminated from the confession. These verses may have been included as a liturgical capping upon the previous sayings against the unfaithful (vv 5-6; 9-10; 11). Having thus delineated the boundaries of the confession, this chapter turns to the content of the confession.

---

[9]Duhm, *Das Buch*, 148, dates this piece in the second century.
[10]For example, Judge, deceitful spring, Tester of mind and heart.

II. ARGUMENT AND PURPOSE OF THE CONFESSION

This confession opens on a more positive note than any other of the confessions. Motifs sounded stridently in the confession of c 15 appear here in a softened, less desperate key. Whereas in 15:18 Jeremiah declared that his wound was "incurable, refusing to be healed," he now proclaims that he would be healed if Yahweh would heal him (17:14a). And what had been a promise of assurance on the part of Yahweh to save the prophet (15:20, cf., 1:18) is here turned into an assertion of the prophet's confidence in Yahweh's power to save him. The prophet claims to have a special relationship with Yahweh; Yahweh is his song of priase, one to whom the prophet is devoted (14c).

The complaint and petition portions of this confession are punctuated by the emphatic use of personal pronouns, "I," "you," "they," which serve to underscore the responsibility of each of the players in the prophet's dilemma. "They," the unidentified enemies, are the proximate cause of the problem which is illustrated by a quotation of their taunting attack upon the prophet. "Where is the word of Yahweh? Let it come." This remark provides the key to the passage and reveals the nature of the prophet's predicament. The prophetic word of judgment, the word of Yahweh which the prophet has been announcing has not yet come to pass.[11] Such a delay in fulfillment of the word means that a distinguishing mark of a true prophet was lacking to Jeremiah because the true prophet's preaching must attain fulfillment.[12] Jeremiah's had not. What is at stake is not only Jeremiah's credibility as Yahweh's true spokesman, but the very word of God which the prophet claimed to speak.

The disbelieving voice of the "they" in the poem is contrasted adversatively to the voice of the "I" (ואני). Jeremiah had never been eager to receive the message he was required to deliver (v 16). In contrast to the enemies who mockingly urge the coming of Yahweh's word, Jeremiah declares his innocence of all desire for its coming and of any implication in the origin of the word. He neither pressed for (לא-אצתי) nor longed for (לא התאויתי) the day of judgment. To make clear his abdication of

---

[11]See Berridge, *Prophet*, 138 and Bright, "Jeremiah's Complaints: Liturgy or Expressions of Personal Distress?" in *Proclamation and Presence: Old Testament Essays in Honor of G. H. Davies*, J. I. Durham and J. R. Porter, eds. (Richmond: John Knox, 1970) 184-214, for a discussion of the language דבר יהוה and בוא. Bright shows that בוא means "come to pass" or "come true" when used of God's word or purpose (see 206).

[12]Cf., Dt 18:22; 28:9.

responsibility for the invention of the word of evil (לרעה)[13] and for the day of judgment (ויום אנוש. literally, "day without cure"), Jeremiah appeals to Yahweh (אתה) who knows (ידעת) everything the prophet has spoken. His words were ever before him (16cd).

The main point of the poem begins to emerge in v 17 where the prophet petitions Yahweh not to be a terror to him (למחתה). Though the nature of this petition is subtle and provocative rather than direct and clear, it can be deduced from the context of the verse that Yahweh would avoid being a terror to the prophet if Yahweh would fulfill the word and thereby deprive the enemies' mocking statements of validity. The motivation offered to Yahweh to actualize the word is the special relationship which exists between God and the prophet. Yahweh is the prophet's refuge on the day of distress (17b). The significance of this appeal to the prophet's relationship with Yahweh is that it establishes grounds for Jeremiah's legitimation as a true prophet.

The petition of v 17 is continued and expanded in v 18. The prophet more specifically indicates how Yahweh should act in order to serve as the prophet's refuge. The enemies (המה), not the prophet (אני), should be ashamed and terrified (יבשו, יחתו) and Yahweh should bring upon them the evil day of judgment. This request for terrifying the enemies employs language of the call narrative but with a surprising twist. In the call account, Yahweh commands Jeremiah not to be terrified before his enemies (the people) lest Yahweh terrify Jeremiah (אל-תחת מפניהב כן- אחתך לפנהם 1:17b). Here, Jeremiah turns the elements of the sentence around and begs Yahweh to terrify the enemies, not the prophet. Consequently, the petition of this confession makes a bold appeal to Yahweh's fidelity to the earlier commitment to the prophet.

The last element of the prophet's request, his call for the coming of the day of judgment, has perplexed a number of scholars. They see in it a contradiction of Jeremiah's assertion in v 16 that he neither desired nor pressed for the "calamitous day." To explain the apparent contradiction between these verses, Rudolph interprets Jeremiah's disclaimer in v 16 as a statement of the prophet's lack of desire for judgment upon all Israel. He then understands v 18 as a request for judgment upon only the

---

[13]See text-critical note.

prophet's personal enemies.[14] Duhm[15] and Cornill[16] take the more drastic measure of striking v 18.

However, properly understood, vv 16 and 18 are not contradictory even if it is assumed that the judgment is directed toward all Israel in both verses. The purpose of v 16 is to establish Jeremiah's innocence of any part in the origination of the message of judgment. Not only did he not invent the word as do false prophets, he wanted nothing whatsoever to do with it. But once the prophetic word was spoken it must come true if it is finally to be recognized as a true word. Vv 17 and 18, and in particular v 18cd, petition Yahweh to vindicate the prophet by bringing about the promised judgment. Only the coming of the evil day would establish Jeremiah as an authentic prophet in the face of the sarcasm of his enemies (v 15). The claim that Jeremiah did not take the initiative in the origination of the message does not contradict his desire for the fulfillment of that message once it was announced.

Jeremiah's third confession begs Yahweh to vindicate the prophetic word and ultimately to vindicate Yahweh by fulfilling that word. At the same time, this confession makes subtle claims that Jeremiah is a true prophet. It begins with a statement that it is within Yahweh's power to end the prophet's ordeal and claims the existence of a special relationship between Jeremiah and Yahweh (v 14). It argues that Jeremiah never had any interest in the message he was required to deliver, making clear that it was not a message of his own invention (15ab). It asserts that Yahweh is a witness to Jeremiah's innocence because the prophet's utterances were all known by Yahweh (16cd).

These conditions of his prophetic life sharply distinguish Jeremiah from the false prophets who never stood in Yahweh's council and who ran to prophesy lies which could never be fulfilled (cf., 23:18ff.; 27-28). These prophets have neither the word nor the support of Yahweh. The major accent of this confession is its call for a vindication of the prophetic message, but in the process of presenting this petition Jeremiah adds strength to his claim to be Yahweh's true prophet.

---

[14]Rudolph, *Jeremia*, 119.
[15]Duhm, *Das Buch*, 149.
[16]Cornill, *Das Buch*, 218.

III. FORM-CRITICAL DESCRIPTION OF
THE CONFESSION

Like the preceding two confessions, Jer 17:14-18 is patterned after the psalm of individual lament. It includes the following components:

      1. Direct address v 14a
      2. Statement of confidence v 14
      3. Complaint v 15
      4. Plea of innocence v 16
      5. Petition vv 17-18

This is the first confession to include among its form-critical components a statement of confidence in Yahweh and even a hint of praise (14). It exhibits nearly the full complement of constitutive elements of the psalm of individual lament. Recalling that the purpose of this form is to express the speaker's confidence in God in the midst of trial and that the statement of confidence and praise were absent from the first two confessions, their presence in this confession marks a change in Jeremiah's prophetic stance before Yahweh. Combined with the diminishment of accusation against Yahweh, this statement of trust suggests an increased certainty on the part of the prophet that the word would be realized.

4

The Fourth Confession:
Jer 18:18–23

TRANSLATION

18:18   And they said "Come, let us plan schemes
against Jeremiah for the law will not perish
from the priest, nor counsel from the sage,
nor the word from the prophet. Come, let us
smite him with the tongue, so we will
no longer have to listen to all those words of his.

18:19   Yahweh, listen carefully to me
and hear out my lawsuit.[1]

18:20   Should evil be rewarded for good?
For they have dug a pit for me.
Remember how I stood before you
to speak good on their behalf,
to turn your anger from them.

18:21   Therefore, give their children over to famine.
Pour them out by the power of the sword.
Let their women be childless and widowed
and their men be killed by pestilence
and their young men be struck down by the sword in war.

18:22   Let a cry for help be heard in their homes,
[2]Yes, bring a raiding party upon them suddenly,
for they have dug a pit[3] to capture me,
and they have hidden a trap for my feet.

18:23   O Yahweh, you know all their schemes for my death.
Do not pardon their iniquity.
Do not blot[4] out their sins from your presence.
Let[5] them be brought to ruin[6] before you.
In the time of your anger act against them.

TEXT-CRITICAL NOTES

18:19   [1] יְרִיבָי is corrected to רִיבִי to follow the LXX.

[2] כי is emphatic, BDB, 472e.

18:22   [3] שׂיחה is corrected to שׂוּחה. See 18:20.

18:23   [4] תֶּמְחִי should be read תְּמַח. See Rudolph, *Jeremiah*, 124.

[5] וְהָיוּ is corrected to the imperative, יְהִי with the LXX.

[6] מַכְשָׁלִים is corrected to מִכְשֹׁלָם to suit the imperative. See BDB, 506.

I. ABSENCE OF CRITICAL PROBLEMS

Of the five confessions found in the Book of Jeremiah, the fourth has received the least attention from scholars. No journal articles on the passage have appeared in recent years. For the most part, treatment of these verses has been perfunctory even in the commentaries.[1] The dearth of scholarly opinion on the passage is probably due to the absence of any serious critical problems such as have plagued the interpretation of the other confessions. The passage moves smoothly in its argument and lacks the sharp contradictions in content commonly found in the other four poems. It is true that the authenticity of vv 21-23 has been called into question on theological grounds. The vengeance requested by the prophet in these verses is excessive. As a result, some see the sentiments as

---

[1] Weiser's commentary presents an admirable exception, *Das Buch*, 162-165.

unfitting for expression by the prophet,[2] but no literary arguments have been advanced to support the elimination of these lines.

II. LITERARY AND STRUCTURAL ANALYSIS OF THE CONFESSION

A literary and structural study of this confession shows that the passage comprises a carefully structured poem (19-23) and editorial prose expansion (v 18).

A. The Poem

Both from the viewpoint of content and from the perspective of structure, the poem may be divided into two strophes, 19-20 and 22-23, with v 21 functioning as a bridge between the two. Each strophe develops its own theme. Vv 19-21 set forth Jeremiah's predicament vis-à-vis his enemies. Vv 21-23 present his petition for a reversal of fate between himself and those enemies. Structurally, the two strophes are formed of parallel elements to create a balanced poetic unity. This balance is achieved by the repetition in the second strophe of words and phrases occurring in a similar location in the first strophe.

In v 19b Jeremiah employs the word שמע to implore Yahweh to listen to his lawsuit; in 22a the prophet again uses שמע (Niph.) in his request that his enemies cry out for help. So too, in 22c the clause כי-כרו שיחה ללכדני,[3] providing Yahweh with motivation for destroying the prophet's antagonists, echoes the prophet's complaint כי-כרו שוחה לנפשי in 20b. In 20c the prophet depicts himself standing before Yahweh (לנפיך) as an intercessor; in 23c,d the contrasting wickedness of the enemies is described in the petitions for their destruction before Yahweh (מלפניך, לפניך). So too, the second strophe closes with the phrase בעת אפך עשה בהם in 23a echoing the end of the first strophe. There Jeremiah reminds Yahweh that he formerly interceded to turn Yahweh's anger away from the enemies להשיב את-חמתך מהם 20e. The following chart illustrates the poetic balance of the poem.

---

[2]Duhm, *Das Buch;* Cornill, *Das Buch,* 227-228.
[3]See text-critical note.

1. 19b	שמע	1. 22a	תשמע
2. 20b	כי-כרו שוחה	2. 22c	כי-כרו שיחה
3. 20c	לפניך	3. 23c,d	לפניך ,מלפניך
4. 20e	-להשיב את	4. 23c	בעת אפך
	המתך מהם		עשה בהם

V 21 which begins Jeremiiah's petition ties these two poetic pieces together. Its introductory לכן indicates that the petition flows logically from Jeremiah's complaint. The rejection and persecution of the prophet demand his vindication. This will occur when his proclaimed word is fulfilled and the nation is destroyed.[4] The conclusion to be drawn from these literary observations is that vv 19-23 form a unified poetic piece. This means that the theological objection to vv 21-23 as too extreme to be appropriate to Jeremiah is completely untenable on literary grounds.

B. The Secondary Insertion: V 18

Upon first reading, v 18 appears integral to the subsequent poem. It is connected to v 19 by the presence of the verb קשב and by its repetition of חשב within the verse. Linguistic repetitions within verses appear to be a characteristic feature of Jeremiah's style in the confessions (e.g., 17:14; 15:19). However, the literary suitability of the verse is not sufficient to warrant its inclusion in the original poem. The verse must be seen as redactional for the following reasons:

    a. V 18 is probably prosaic, but even if it is not, its lines are considerably longer and less balanced than those of the poem.

    b. The only linguistic link between v 18 and the poem is the verb which occurs again in v 19.

    c. The use of the proper name Jeremiah in v 18 is unusual. When Jeremiah is referred to within quotations of enemies elsewhere in the

---

[4]See Rudolph, *Jeremia*, 125, and Weiser, *Das Buch*, 164-165. Combined with the two following verses, v 21 has evoked strong attacks from the commentators on theological grounds. Some wish to discredit the verse altogether as unworthy of the prophet because of the excessive vengeance it calls down upon the enemies. Others use it to underline a supposed difference between the two testaments—an Old Testament ethic of rampant vengeance against the enemy set against a New Testament ethic of Christian love of the enemy. But such interpretations facilely overstate ethical distance between the two testaments.

confessions, he is always mentioned without the use of the proper name (cf., 11:19; 17:15; 20:10).

d. The content of this verse is similar to that of 11:21-23, another redactional insertion. In both insertions the enemies deliberately refuse to listen to the prophetic word. (See Chapter 1.)

e. As in other redactional additions to the confessions (11:21-23 and 12:6),[5] this verse functions midrashically, that is, it explicitly identifies the problem and the enemies left unidentified by the confession.

f. Again like the redactional insertion of 11:21-23, this verse forms a self-contained literary unit. It is composed of three parallel phrases and is framed by לכן followed by a first person plural verb. This means that v 18 can be removed from the context without harm to itself or to the poem which follows. V 18, therefore, serves as an introduction to the confession and shows that the theological issue at the level of the redaction is the continuation of the prophetic word.[6]

III. THE ARGUMENT AND PURPOSE
OF THE CONFESSION

In its original form the five-verse poem differs from the first two confessions (11:18ff., and 15:10ff.) in two ways. First, it is less concerned with the persecution of the prophet, mentioning his suffering only in 20b, 22cd, 23a, and more concerned with petition for God's intervention. Second, although accusation against Yahweh remains an element of the confession, at best it is subtle and indirect. In these two respects, this confession continues the shift away from angry complaint and accusation of the first and second confessions toward increased confidence in Yahweh, already noted in the third confession.

V 19 opens the poem in typical confessional style with the presentation of an abrupt and mysterious circumstance. Jeremiah is appealing urgently (הקשיבו) to Yahweh to hear his lawsuit, but the opponent in the suit is not clear. Introducing what seems at first merely a rhetorical problem, v 20 brings little clarity. "Should evil be paid as if it were good?" With equal mysteriousness, unidentified enemies are introduced and accused of digging a pit for the prophet. Yahweh is reminded of how Jeremiah stood

---

[5]And 11:17, although not itself part of a confession.

[6]See Duhm, *Das Buch,* 156 and Thiel, *Die deuteronomistische Redaktion* I, 217-218, who also recognizes the redactional nature of this verse.

before him (זכר עמדי לכניך),[7] a prophet interceding for the good of the enemy to avert Yahweh's judgment. Clearly, the question of v 20a is not theoretical but practical. It arises from the prophet's concrete dilemma—his enemies appear triumphant while he encounters only derision.

Composed entirely of petition, the second part of the poem (vv 21-23), contrasts the fate desired for the enemy with Jeremiah's plight (vv [18] 19-20). Jeremiah asks that the enemies also be heard, but not their prayers; instead, cries of distress when the marauders come upon them (22b). The enemies deserve their fate (v 21) because of their attempts to take the life of Yahweh's prophet. Jeremiah begs Yahweh not to act in the characteristic mode of forgiveness (23bc) but to bring judgment against them (23de).

Initially, Jeremiah's opponent in the *rîb* appears to be the enemies who seek to destroy him and about whom he appeals to Yahweh, the Just Judge (11:20), for revenge. Yet considering Jeremiah's previous attack upon the righteousness of the Righteous Judge (12:1-3), his lawsuit is probably again directed against Yahweh. It is Yahweh who is in control of events and it is Yahweh who can repay the behavior of people and prophet with justice or injustice. Yahweh is a witness to the wickedness of the enemy and knows all their schemes to obliterate the prophet (23a). Yahweh alone can avenge Jeremiah.

Despite these elements of expostulation, angry accusations against Yahweh are firmly curtailed in this confession compared to those of the first two. In this poem, indictment is only implied. Emphasis is rather upon the prophet's petition for judgment. But this request is no mere "human" wish for vengeance as distinguished from the purer and holier desires suitable to a prophet. It is a request that the word of Yahweh, expressed through the prophet, be fulfilled in the face of all nefarious threats against it.

Should it not already be clear from the poem itself that the real issue of this confession is the vindication of the prophetic word, the redactional addition makes the matter explicit. In v 18 the enemies are identified as those who want to hear no more of Jeremiah's words (ואל-נקשיבה אל-כל-דבריו).[8] The message of the prophet reported from the beginning of the Book was finally and totally rejected by all the people in 18:12. It is the

---

[7]Cf., 15:19 where the language of "standing before Yahweh" is also used.

[8]This verse provides an apt description of the state of Israel's religious institutions during the Exile.

report of this rejection which explains the intensity of the prophet's call for vengeance, the most extensive and embittered in all of Jeremiah.

IV. FORM-CRITICAL DESCRIPTION
OF THE CONFESSION

The form-critical components of this confession are:

1. Direct Address v 19
2. Complaint vv 20ab, 22cd, 23a
3. Plea of innocence v 20cde
4. Petition for intervention vv 21-23

Form-critically, the fourth confession follows the same format as the first two confessions. Again lacking are the constitutive elements of the statement of confidence and the vow of praise. Despite this similarity among the components of the three confessions, the element of petition dominates this confession alone.

5

The Fifth Confession:
Jer 20:7–13(18)

TRANSLATION

20:7   You deceived[1] me, Yahweh, and I was deceived.
You were stronger than I and you prevailed.
I have become a laughingstock every day.
Everyone mocks me.

20:8   (For) whenever I speak, I must cry out,
I must shout,[2] "Violence and ruin!"
For the word of Yahweh has become for me
A reproach and a derision every day.

20:9   Whenever I think, "I will not remember him,
I will speak[3] no longer in his name,"
Then it is like a fire consuming my heart, shut up[4] in my bones.
I become weary holding it in and I cannot.

20:10   I heard the whispering of the crowd,
"'Terror on every side,' proclaim,[5] let us proclaim for him."
All my friends are watching for me to stumble.
"Perhaps he will be deceived and we will prevail
And we will take our vengeance upon him."

20:11   But Yahweh is with me as a Mighty Warrior.
Therefore my pursuers will stumble and they will not prevail.
Because they will not succeed,
They will be shamed with an eternal humiliation which will
    not be forgotten.

20:12   O Yahweh,[6] Tester of the righteous,[7]
Who sees the heart and the mind,
Let me see your vengeance upon them
Because to you I have made known my cause.

20:13   Sing to Yahweh, praise him,[8]
For he has rescued the life of the needy from the hand of
      evildoers.

20:14   Cursed is the day on which I was born.
The day on which my mother bore me, let it not be blessed.

20:15   Cursed is the man[9] who brought the news to my father saying,
"A son is born to you," making him very glad.

20:16   Let[10] that man be like the cities which the Lord destroyed
      without pity.
Let him hear[11] the war cry in the morning and the alarm at
      noon.

20:17   Because he did not kill me in the womb[12]
So that my mother would have become my grave
And her womb be pregnant forever.

20:18   Why did I come forth from the womb
To see trouble and grief and to end my days in shame?

TEXT-CRITICAL NOTES

20:7   [1]For the translation of פתה see below.

20:8   [2]Both J. Muilenburg, Commentary, 2, and the JPS aptly translate אקרא as "shout."

20:9   [3] ואמרתי denotes the frequentive past action which is continued
by ולא with the imperfect, GKC, 112kk.

      [4]Some scholars unnecessarily emend עצר to a feminine form to
make it agree with כאש, but when two adjectives follow a

feminine sometimes only the first word takes the feminine,
GKC, 132d.

20:10   [5]The traditional translation of הגידו ונגידנו is "Denounce, let
us denounce him," but nowhere else does נגד carry this negative
meaning. A few translate the word "announce." See W. E.
Nägelsback, "The Prophet Jeremiah," Lang's Commentary on
Holy Scripture (Grand Rapids: Zondervan, 1960) 186 and S. H.
Blank, *Jeremiah: Man and Prophet* (Cincinnati: Hebrew Union
College Press) 1961, 116. "Proclaim," However, suits the
prophetic context better. The suffix of ונגידנו is here construed as the old dative ending, suggested by W. Holladay in a
private conversation. See GKC, 117x.

20:12   [6] צבאות is omitted following the LXX. See 11:20, text-critical
note 7.

[7]It is not necessary to emend צדיק to צדק to make it agree with
its alleged doublet, 11:20, but see below.

20:13   [8]For את-יהוה the LXX reads αὐτῷ. Janzen, *Studies*, 74, has
argued persuasively that this is an example of the MT's propen-
sity to correct the superior LXX toward explicitness.

20:15   [9] האיש is often emended to היוב to continue the thought of the
preceding verse, but the text makes best sense as it is. See
below.

20:16   [10] והיה is corrected to יהי following the LXX.

20:16   [11] ושמע is corrected to ישמע following the LXX.

20:17   [12] מרחם is emended to ברחם following the LXX and the Syriac.
M. Dahood's suggestion in "Denominative *rihham*, 'to conceive,
enwomb,'" *Bib* 44 (1963) 204-205, that מרחם may be a
denominative participle from רחם in the manner of Ugaritic
denominative verbs derived from parts of the body appears
overly complicated and results in an awkward sentence. רחב
usually construed as masculine, is construed here as feminine,
Jouon, 118h.

I. THE PROBLEM OF THE UNITY
OF THE TEXT

In addition to the usual exegetical problems accompanying the Jeremianic confessions, Jer 20:7-18 presents the particular difficulty of apparent
disunity of content. Traditionally regarded as a unit unto itself, the apparent abrupt and contradictory swings in mood expressed in this passage
have caused a number of scholars to question the correctness of viewing it
as a unified whole. No firm consensus exists regarding either the identification of its component elements or the relationship of the elements to
one another. For many scholars, the contrasts of emotion from helplessness (vv 7-10), to trusting confidence (vv 11-13), to despair (vv 14-18) are
too sharp to have been present in an original literary unity.

Some, therefore, divide the text into three discrete literary units
understood to correspond to the prophet's moods at different moments in
his career.[1] They buttress this position by an appeal to the text's literary
features such as the repetition of words in vv 7 and 10 and vv 14 and 18
and the supposedly balanced meter of certain lines.[2] Others attempt to
resolve the difficulty by eliminating, according to a variety of criteria,
some or all of these verses. Cornill, for instance, eliminates v 11 for
metrical and linguistic reasons;[3] others strike v 12 as a doublet of 11:20;[4]
and still others remove v 13 because of its psalm-like language and style.[5]

---

[1]These units are 7-10, 11-13 and 14-18. See D. F. Giesebrecht, *Das
Buch*, 11-114; J. R. Lundblom, *Jeremiah: A Study in Ancient Hebrew
Rhetoric*, SBLDS 18 (Missoula: Scholars Press, 1975) 45-47; Condamin, *Le
Livre*, 160-165.

[2]Lundblom, *Jeremiah*, 45-47 and Condamin, *Le Livre*, 165.

[3]In D. C. Cornill's view, *Das Buch*, 238, גבור עריץ is not a Jeremianic expression.

[4]H. Wildberger, *Jahwewort und prophetische Rede bei Jeremia*, Diss #2
(Zurich: Zwingli, 1942) 90; Cornill, *Das Buch*, 238; J. P. Hyatt, "The Book
of Jeremiah," *IB* 5 (Nashville: Abingdon, 1956) 973; Stanley Marrow,
"*Hamas* in Jer 20:8," *VD* 43 (1965) 241; Duhm, *Das Buch*, 166.

[5]Duhm, *Das Buch*, 166; Condamin, *Le Livre*, 165; Cornill, *Das Buch*,
238; Wildberger, *Jahwewort*, 90; Hyatt, *IB* 5, 974. In addition C. Westermann classifies v 13 as an "eschatological song of praise," a form which
mixes prophetic and psalmic content and form, and so he treats it as a
separate unit. *The Praise of God in the Psalms* (Richmond: John Knox,
1965) 142. H. Gunkel, *Einleitung in die Psalmen* (Göttingen: Vandenhoeck
& Ruprecht, 1933) 172, and J. M. Berridge, *Prophet* disagree with all these
positions claiming that vv 11-13, introduced by v 10, form the original
lament of Jeremiah to which vv 7-9 and 14-18 were later added.

The psychological content of vv 14-18 similarly casts suspicion upon the genuineness and positioning of these verses. Graf disputes their authenticity because the blasphemous content is unworthy of the prophet.[6] Michaelis judges vv 14-18 to be a later imitation of Job 3 and, thus, non-Jeremianic.[7] Ewald assails the placement of these verses arguing that vv 14-18 belong more logically prior to vv 7-13.[8] After removing vv 11-13 as indicated above, Cornill claims that vv 14-18 belong immediately after vv 7-10 where they complete Jeremiah's despairing lament.[9]

Obviously, the psychological content of the various components of the passage has provided the principal analytical criterion in its exegesis. Linguistic, literary and form-critical criteria have been granted a subordinate role at best. They have been used primarily to confirm interpretations based on psychological grounds.[10] Until recently Rudolph alone rejected such a method of interpretation.[11] Rudolph contends that the psychology of Jeremiah is unknowable and, therefore, psychological criteria are not adequate for determining the text's unity. Rudolph makes little use of literary or form-critical criteria in approaching the question. He simply treats the entire chapter as a unified whole notwithstanding his recognition that vv 11-13 differ from the surrounding verses.

Such disagreement among scholars concerning the component elements of the text and their relationship to one another has naturally had its consequences for the interpretation of the passage. There has been little agreement regarding its purpose and function beyond the general observation that it provides biographical insight into the spiritual and psychological struggles of the prophet.

---

[6]K. H. Graf, *Der Prophet*, 282.

[7]Michaelis, *Observationes*, 282.

[8]H. Ewald, *Prophets of the Old Testament*, 4 vols. (Edinburgh: Williams and Norgate, 1878) 3, 279.

[9]Cornill, *Das Buch*, 238.

[10]Baumgartner, *Die Klagegedichte*, 48-51; Berridge, *Prophet*, 180; and G. Von Rad, "Die Konfessionen Jeremias," 270-272, for example, include form-critical analyses in their treatments of the confession but none of them is able to account for all the verses in the passage. Weiser's approach is a notable exception, but even he needs to rearrange the verses in order to explain the passage, *Das Buch* 1, 175-177.

[11]Rudolph, *Jeremias*, 129-133; in a recent article, J. A. Clines and D. M. Gunn also argue that no insight whatsoever can be gained into the prophet's personal experience from any part of this passage, "Form, Occasion and Redaction in Jeremiah 20," *ZAW* 88 (1976) 390-409.

Much previous treatment of Jer 20:7-18, therefore, has applied psychological criteria to literary material. Scholars have assumed that the psychology of the prophet is the determining feature for the text's interpretation. Unlike previous chapters in this study, this chapter begins with a form-critical analysis because, in this case, form-critical criteria are essential for determining the perimeters of the confession.

II. 20:7-13: A CONFESSION OF PRAISE

Though a number of scholars consider vv 7-10 and vv 11-13 as separate and unrelated literary pieces, there is a strong form-critical argument for treating these seven verses as a literary unit. The argument derives from a comparative study of the formal components of vv 7-13 and the conventional components of the psalm of individual lament. (vv 14-18 will be treated below.)

In the Jeremiah passage, v 7 opens with a direct address to Yahweh (v 7a), which is incorporated into a description of Jeremiah's predicament (vv 7-10). This predicament includes Yahweh's treatment of Jeremiah (v 7a,b), the actions of Jeremiah's enemies against him (vv 7cd, 10), Jeremiah's own actions and their consequences (v 8), and Jeremiah's internal struggles (v 9). Connected to the preceding verses by the *waw* adversative, v 11 switches abruptly to a statement of confidence in Yahweh's saving presence, followed by a description of the expected results of that presence (v 11b,cd). An immediately following address to Yahweh, v 12 includes a description of Yahweh's actions and a petition for vengeance upon Jeremiah's enemies (bc). V 13 ends the unit with a command to praise Yahweh (13a) and with a general reason for that praise (v 13b). The formal components of the text are:

1. Invocation (v 7a)
2. Description of the predicament of the speaker (vv 7-10)
3. Confession of confidence (v 11)
4. Petition (v 12)
5. Command to praise (v 13)

Precisely these elements constitute the classic form of the psalm of individual lament. (See Chapter 1.) It is true that Jer 20:7-13 lacks three elements of the ideal form and contains a variation of another element of the ideal form.[12] But it is also true that psalm forms never became so stereotyped in Israel as to exclude variation in the number and arrangement of elements.[13] With the exception of the vow of praise, Jer 20:7-13 includes all the constituent features of the form, including the *waw* adversative connection of the confession of confidence to the description of the predicament.[14]

In this passage the vow of praise has been replaced by a command to praise (v 13). But Westermann has demonstrated that a whole group of individual laments omit the vow of praise entirely (Pss 38, 141, 143); other psalms change the vow of praise into a statement of praise (Pss 6:5; 17:15; 73:28; 88:10-12) and, of most importance for Jer 20:7-13, other laments change the vow of praise into an exhortation to praise (Pss 27:15; 31:24; while Ps 22:24 includes an imperative along with the vow of priase).[15] Form-critically, therefore, Jer 20:7-13 contains a single literary unit, a psalm of individual lament.[16]

Linguistic patterns within the passage provide ample support for this analysis. First, within individual verses of the lament, a stylistic pattern of repeated words appears:

פתיתני . . . ואפת	in v 7
אדבר, דבר יהוה, אדבר	in vv 8,9
הגידו ונגידנו	in v 10
ראה אראה	in v 12[17]

Second, across the verses of the lament, a fairly complicated, unifying pattern of repetitions is present:

---

[12]The missing elements are: assurance of being heard, wish for God's intervention, direct praise of God. The variation is that a command to praise is substituted for the vow of praise, Westermann, *The Praise*, 64.

[13]A. Weiser, *The Psalms: A Commentary* SBL (Philadelphia: Fortress, 1962) 69.

[14]Westermann, *The Praise*, 64.

[15]Ibid., 75, n. 24.

[16]This decision was reached independently of the work of Clines and Gunn (see note 2).

[17]If one follows the MT, the word Yahweh is also repeated (v 13), but this repetition appears qualitatively different from the others.

Appearing in vv 7b and 8b, כל-היום joins the two verses. פתה and יכל occurring in v 7a and v 10c, form a linguistic frame enclosing the statement of predicament of the psalm. יכל moreover, turns up again in vv 9c and 11a, while נקמתנו ממנו at the end of v 10c form a linguistic frame with נקמתך מהם in v 12b, connecting the praise portion of the psalm with the lament portion.

By suggesting that an intentional literary activity underlies them, these stylistic features of repetition within verses, plus the interlocking patterns of repetition across the verses, add weight to the form-critical argument that Jer 20:7-13 is a single literary unit.

The correctness of this analysis seems all the more probable when one joins to it an awareness of significant weaknesses in the arguments for the elimination of vv 11-13 presented above. Cornill's claim, for instance, that v 11 does not fit with the preceding verses because it is not metrical, can be disqualified on two grounds. First, in a study of meter in Hebrew poetry, D. K. Stuart[18] has shown that Hebrew poetry does not follow a rigid metrical pattern. It frequently alternates long and short cola and balanced and unbalanced meter without clear design. Stuart proposes that these sudden rhythmical variations may function to introduce an element of surprise or emphasis at certain points in the poetry. If Stuart's arguments are correct, metrical reasons are not sufficient for removing v 11 from the passage. Second, even if Stuart's arguments were to be found wanting, the metrical argument still lacks force because the surrounding verses do not yield a uniform metrical pattern whether one counts accents or one counts syllables.[19]

The claim that v 12 is a doublet of 11:20, and hence, should be removed from the confession is significantly weakened by a close examination of the first line of the two verses (20:12 and 11:20). The most striking difference between the two results from their use of verbs. The first verb of 11:20, שׁפט is lacking in 20:12, while the second verb of 11:20, בהן serves as the first verb of 20:12. The second verb of 20:12 ראה seems to be taken from the following line to create a stylistic pattern similar to other verses in the psalm. (See above.)

---

[18]D. K. Stuart, *Studies in Early Hebrew Meter*, HSM, 13 (Missoula: Scholars Press, 1976).

[19]Cornill's linguistic argument that בגור עריץ is not a Jeremianic term (see note 4) is incorrect. עריץ appears in 15:21 and גבור occurs five other times in the Book and is applied specifically to Yahweh in 14:9.

Another difference between the two verses is found in the objects of the participles. In 20:12 the object is the adjective צדיק while in 11:20 the object is the noun צדק. Scribal activity might explain these variations. Nonetheless, the differences between the two lines are sufficient to suggest other possibilities such as an original *Vorlage*, perhaps a cultic prayer, underlying both texts. Without further evidence, of course, proposals regarding the origin of these two verses remain purely speculative. What is important for the argument of this paper is simply the recognition that the differences between the two verses are sufficient to make the retention of both a thoroughly reasonable procedure.[20]

Finally, the contention that v 13 should be omitted because it is psalm-like in style and language merely strengthens the form-critical argument advanced above.[21] Arguments for the elimination of these three verses, therefore, have little force, while form-critical and literary considerations provide strong reasons for viewing the passage as a literary unity.

If this analysis of Jer 20:7-13 is correct, two consequences follow for the interpretation of the passage. First, to explain the coexistence of two contradictory psychological moods in the text it is unnecessary to subdivide the passage, to eliminate verses, or to speculate about Jeremiah's psychological fitness.[22] It is characteristic of the psalms of individual lament to move from statements of distress in tragic predicaments to sudden bursts of confidence and trust in the midst of that predicament. Second, the general purpose of the psalm of individual lament is to express confidence in Yahweh's help in the midst of suffering.[23] In this text, then, one need not see two distinct purposes arising from two separate historical moments in the prophet's life. There is one general intention—to proclaim Jeremiah's full confidence that Yahweh is with him and will act for him despite all appearances to the contrary.

---

[20]See Marx, "A propos des doublets," 107 and Hubman, *Exkurs: Die Doppelüberlieferungen (DÜ) im Jer-buch,* 217-244.

[21]One reason frequently given for the rejection of the verse is the presence of the word אביון, a favorite word of the Psalmist, but this word is employed also in Jer 2:34; 5:8 and 26:16.

[22]For example, see McNamara, "Jeremia," NCCHS (London: Nelson & Sons, 1969) 113.

[23]Weiser, *Psalms,* 81-82.

III. ARGUMENT AND PURPOSE
OF THE CONFESSION

The first problem confronting the interpreter of Jer 20:7-13 is how to translate the opening line of v 7. The difficulty arises from the verb פתה. A number of scholars translate the first clause as "You seduced me, Yahweh, and I was seduced." Some even propose that this sexual motif, initiated by פתה, is extended in the passage by חזק and חמס ושד.[24] However, of the many uses of פתה in the Old Testament there are only three texts where the word must be translated with a sexual connotation (Ex 22:15; Hos 2:14; Jb 31:9 in the niphal). A close reading of these shows that the sexual meaning emerges from the contexts and not from the verb itself.

פתה may carry a sexual nuance in one other Old Testament text (Ju 14:15; 16:5), the story of Samson and Delilah. However, the primary meaning of the word in this passage is "to deceive" or "to trick" Samson into revealing the secret of his strength. In a few places, the verb also denotes enticement or temptation in a general sense with no reference to sex (Pro 1:10; 16:29). By far the most common use of פתה is "to deceive" by means of a direct lie (Pro 24:28; 1 Kgs 22:20, 21, 22; and parallel text, 2 Chron 18:19-21; Ps 78:36), or by means of an implied lie (2 Sam 3:25; Ezek 14:9, where it is used twice).[25]

The subsequent verbs in v 7 also do not require a translation in sexual terms. There are only six instances, all in the hiphil stem, where חזק carries a sexual connotation (Dt 22:25; Pro 7:13; Isa 4:1; 2 Sam 13:11; Ju 19:25, 29), but in Jer 20:7 חזק appears in the Qal stem. Nowhere in Qal or Piel stems does חזק have anything to do with sexual imagery. Instead, it conveys the basic idea of strength modified according to a variety of situations: military strength (2 Kgs 3:26; 14:5; 2 Chr 26:15; 28:20; Josh 17:13; 1 Kgs 20:23); moral strength, power, superior strength (Gen 41:57; 47:20; Mal 3:13; 2 Sam 16:21; Josh 23:6; 1 Kgs 20:20, 25); hardening of Pharaoh's heart (Ex 7:13, 22; 8:15; 9:35; 12:33).[26] It appears likely, then,

---

[24]Bright, AB 129; Marrow, "*Hamas* in Jer 20:8"; Condamin, *Le Livre*, 160; Berridge, *Prophet,* 151-153.

[25]Against Clines and Gunn, who deny that deceit is the primary meaning of the word, "'You Tried to Persuade Me' and 'Violence and Outrage'" in Jeremiah XX:7-8," *VT* 28 (1978) 20-271.

[26]חמס ושד as the cry of a raped woman occurs nowhere in the OT but is only imagined as the expression she would have called in Dt 22:27 had it been recorded. See Berridge, *Prophet,* 153-154.

that finding sexual imagery in this passage stems from a generalization of a few isolated uses of פתה and חזק and from a failure to consider the context of Jer 20:7.[27] These arguments aside, however, the poetic nature of the material may signal that all ranges of meaning are being invoked by the use of richly nuanced language.[28]

In prophetic literature there are two uses of the word פתה, which provide further insight into the connotations of the word for Jer 20:7 and 11. In Ezek 14:9 the false prophet is deceived (יפתה) directly by Yahweh (פתיתי). In 1 Kgs 22:20-22 (cf. the parallel, 1 Chron 18:19-21), Yahweh is assisted in the deception of the false prophets by a lying spirit which Yahweh puts into the mouth of the prophets (1 Kgs 22:23). In Jeremiah's lament, though the grammatical construction is different, a similar accusation of deception by Yahweh is uttered by the prophet. Moreover, in both passages פתה is used in close association with יכל (cf., also 20:11).[29]

These contextual similarities suggest that in Jer 20:7, 11 פתה includes the meaning "to deceive" with the special nuance given it in the other two prophetic texts. Jeremiah is accusing Yahweh of deceiving him as a prophet, making him a false prophet by sheer domination, יכל, and superior strength, חזק. In Jeremiah's battle with Yahweh, Yahweh is the stronger and overpowers him as the lying spirit had overpowered the prophets of Ahab. This representation of Yahweh appears to reverse the prophet's relationship with God inaugurated at his commissioning. In c 1 Yahweh had promised that although all the land fight against Jeremiah, they would not prevail, יכל (1:8). Yahweh would be with him to deliver him. Now, however, Yahweh is cast as Jeremiah's deceitful opponent.

But it is not simply Jeremiah's proclamation that Yahweh is his adversary that prompts the lament. Jeremiah also complains that he is daily a

---

[27]Perhaps a reason commentators have found this translation attractive is that the presence of a seduction motif would help underscore the intimate and violent nature of Jeremiah's spiritual struggle with Yahweh which the passage is alleged to depict.

[28]For such a view of Hebrew poetry see Gerhard von Rad, *Old Testament Theology*, II, D. M. G. Stalker, trans. (New York: Harper & Row, 1965) 84.

[29]In 1 Kgs 22:20-23, Yahweh asks who will deceive (יפתה) the prophets. Yahweh commands the volunteer to put a lying spirit into the mouth of the prophets. You are to deceive him (תפתה) and you will succeed (וגם-תוכל). But in Jer 20:7, the prophet accuses Yahweh of deceiving him (פתיתני יהוה ואפת) and Yahweh succeeds (ותוכל).

laughingstock, mocked by everyone. The relationship of these two complaints to one another is not made clear until v 8. Syntactically connected to v 7 by the introductory כי and linguistically connected by the repeated phrase כל-היום, v 8 implicitly links Yahweh's alleged deceit to the mockery of Jeremiah's enemies. Jeremiah has become a laughingstock because of the offensive contents of his prophetic message. In this verse the prophetic nature of Jeremiah's mission is emphasized by the use of three different verbs of speaking (אדבר, אזעק, אקרא). The second verb, זעק, which often expresses a cry that precedes the coming of calamity or destruction,[30] introduces the content of Jeremiah's message by immediately preceding it. The message itself is a message of judgment, חמס ושד, "violence and ruin," and is here the direct object of the three verbs. An expression conveying several nuances, the prophetic pronouncement of חמס ושד promises that Judah will experience physical violence, perversion of justice and violation of law. In other words, general chaos and destruction will come.[31]

In a recent article, J. A. Clines and D. M. Gunn have argued, however, that חמס ושד refers exclusively to Jeremiah's anger at Yahweh for forcing him to prophesy.[32] Contextual considerations indicate the unlikeliness of this interpretation. First, the double כי and the double use of דבר in v 8 imply that the subject of 8c is synonymous with the object of 8ab and, therefore, both חמס ושד and דבר יהוה refer to Jeremiah's message. Second, the antecedent of ויהוה בלבי יכאש בערת in 9c is the דבר יהוה of 8c.

This comparison of the word of Yahweh with fire emphasizes the wrathful content of both Yahweh's word and the message of Jeremiah. In 5:14 the prophets speak falsely, denying the judgment about to come upon the people. As a consequence, Yahweh promises that the divine word will be a fire of judgment in Jeremiah's mouth (cf. 23:29). In 6:11 Jeremiah uses the phrase נלאיתי הכיל, to describe his inability to hold in the wrath of Yahweh, ונלאיתי כלכל (20:9c). These linguistic considerations imply that the word of Yahweh in 20:9 is a word of wrath.

---

[30]Cf., 11:11, 12; 47:2; 25:35; 48:20, 31; 30:15. Clines and Gunn, "You Tried to Persuade Me," 77, contend that זעק is a technical term for the cry of the oppressed, in this case, Jeremiah, but see 48:20, 31; 25:34; 47:2; 11:11, where זעק is used as a cry before war and calamity with no reference to unjust oppression.

[31]See Marrow, "Ḥamas in Jer 20:8," n. 28.

[32]Clines and Gunn, "You Tried to Persuade Me," 26; and "Form, Occasion and Redaction," 395.

Third, in 10b the crowd mocks Jeremiah by mimicking his message of
חמס ושד, with the terror-filled epithet, מבור מסביב.[33] Thus, חמס ושד and
מגור מסביב also function as synonyms for Jeremiah's message. If these
observations are correct, the content of Jeremiah's message is at issue in
8b,c; 9c and 10b. This message is the cause of mockery by his enemies and
provokes his accusation that Yahweh has deceived him (7ab).

A glance at cc 1-20 confirms Jeremiah's assessment of the content of
his message as חמס ושד. His prophecy has promised violence and
destruction upon Judah and Jerusalem (10:22; 4:13-17), upon priest and
prophets (6:13-15; 8:8-12), upon king and people (2:2-8; 14:16) and even
upon the land itself (14:2-6). And this message of violence and ruin is
Yahweh's word.

V 9, tied to v 8 by the repetition of the word דבר, describes Jeremiah's
unsuccessful attempt to extricate himself from the predicament wrought
by the preaching of this message. He tries not to remember Yahweh, the
source of his prophetic speech, nor to speak any longer in Yahweh's name.
These persistent efforts reveal Jeremiah's emphatic desire to turn his
back upon his prophetic task. His efforts are futile. He is completely helpless,[34] overpowered by the one who is stronger and overwhelmed by the
divine word as by an uncontrollable fire. Jeremiah lives under an inescap-
able compulsion to proclaim the message of judgment.

Linked to the preceding verse by the כי of 10a, v 10 frames the whole
lament portion of the psalm of lament both by the repetition of the mocking theme (7c,d) and by the linguistic frame which יפתה ונוכלה of 10c
forms with 7a. Alternating comments of Jeremiah with his quotations of
the words of the crowd, v 10 draws a dramatic picture of Jeremiah over-
hearing the crowd's mockery.[35] Jeremiah, first, reports the crowd's
mimicry of his message, "Terror on every side." Then, in an aside, he identifies the taunting rabble as "his friends" who seek his downfall. Next, he
quotes them again as they express their hope that Jeremiah would be
deceived as a false prophet, פתה, and that they will be able to overpower
him.

---

[33] Against Bright 132, n. 10, who believes the expression is a mocking
nickname for Jeremiah, and with W. L. Holladay, "The Covenant with the
Patriarchs Overturned: Jeremiah's Intention in 'Terror on Every Side' (Jer
20:1-6," *JBL* 91 (1972) 305-320.
[34] As the JPSV aptly translates יכל in this verse.
[35] This style of abrupt change of speaker is not unusual in the Book of
Jeremiah. Cf., for example, 3:22-23; 5:6-7; 6:9-10; 8:13-14; 10:22-23;
11:19-20; 15:17-18, 19-20.

The expression אנוש שלומי with which Jeremiah describes his enemies has been identified as an idiom expressing close friendship as in Ps 41:10.[36] In light of the poetic nature of the text, the expression may contain another nuance. The word שלום occurs frequently in Jeremiah as the content of the message of the false prophets who say "peace, peace, when there is no peace" (6:14 and its doublet, 8:11; 9:7; 23:17; 28:9). It is possible that this phrase serves as Jeremiah's own term of derision for the false prophets and their message.[37] If this is correct, his friends of peace would really be his enemies of peace who preach a competing prophetic message, one which is the opposite of his message of judgment. They would have every reason to hope for the suppression of Jeremiah's preaching by having him identified as a false prophet. Though the linguistic evidence is too skimpy to assert this suggestion with assurance, the possibility is provocative in the context.

In the last line of v 10 the desires of the crowd coincide with the alleged offense committed against Jeremiah by Yahweh (v 7). The issue raised by these two framing verses is again the legitimacy of Jeremiah's prophecy, a concern raised by both Jeremiah and his enemies. Enclosed by this linguistic and thematic frame, vv 8 and 9 address the same issue. In them it is asserted that the message of violence and ruin proclaimed by Jeremiah is the word of Yahweh (v 8), preached under the force of irresistible compulsion (v 9).

At the end of the description of the predicament (7-10) one has the suspicion that Jeremiah does not genuinely believe Yahweh has deceived him. It may appear so to his contemporaries who desire only a message of security and welfare. It may even appear so at times to Jeremiah himself who must undergo suffering and humiliation for the sake of his mission. Nonetheless, this picture of the suffering prophet in conflict with Yahweh and an object of scorn to his contemporaries makes a subtle claim for the authenticity of Jeremiah's prophetic mission.

---

[36]BDB, 1023. See Jer 38:28 where the same phrase occurs in a poem quite similar to this one and admits of an interpretation such as this paper proposes for its use in 20:10. See below. This text also uses פתה and יכל.

[37]The problem of false prophecy shows up in all the Jeremianic sources leaving little doubt that this phenomenon created a major problem for Jeremiah's life. See I. Meyer, *Jeremia und die Falschen Propheten* (Orbis Biblicus et Orientalis 13; Göttingen: Vandenhoeck & Ruprecht, 1977); and I. Meyer and F. L. Hossfeld, *Prophet Gegen Prophet: Eine Analyse der Alttestamentlichen Texte zum Thema: wahre und falsche Propheten* BB 9 (Fribourg: Schweizerisches Katholisches Bibelwerk, 1973).

This understanding of the complaint portion of the psalm of individual lament gains strength from a consideration of the confession's remaining components (11-13). These verses all express Jeremiah's absolute reliance upon Yahweh who will listen to his cause, take vengeance upon his enemies and vindicate him before them. Despite all appearances to the contrary, Yahweh is with him (v 11) as promised (1:18, 19; 15:20, and cf., 42:11). This powerful presence of Yahweh, כגבור עריץ, will bring about a reversal of fortunes for both Jeremiah and his enemies. Jeremiah will not stumble (10c). It is they who will stumble and fall (11b). The enemies will not prevail (11b). Only Yahweh will prevail.

Jeremiah's certainty that Yahweh knows heart and mind, and so can discern the true from the false (12ab) serves as the ground of his petition for vengeance (12c), נקמתך מהם. The literary frame which this petition forms with 10c, נקמתנו ממנו, indicates that the enemies in question are Jeremiah's "friends," perhaps the false prophets who speak only words of welfare and security. In the reversal of fortunes about to take place the enemies will be discredited and disgraced. Jeremiah and his message of judgment will be fulfilled because Jeremiah is Yahweh's prophet. This psalm of individual lament is, therefore, aptly termed a confession. It praises Yahweh's fidelity and saving power in the midst of the woeful circumstances of Jeremiah's prophetic life.

IV. 20:14-18: THE CURSING POEM

Though scholars frequently question the genuineness of vv 14-18 and their placement within the chapter, few dispute the literary unity of this small passage. Vv 14-18 are marked off from the surrounding material by three features: their formal components, a linguistic framing device and self-containment of content. A composite of literary forms, which is, nonetheless, a single unit, this passage combines the formal elements of a compound curse (vv 14-17)[38] and a concluding non-cultic cry of lament (v 18).[39] It is further distinguished from the surrounding material by the

---

[38]S. H. Blank, "The Curse, the Blasphemy, the Spell, the Oath," HUCA 23/1 (1950-51) 73-76.

[39]Like v 18, Gen 25:22; 27:46; Job 3:15; 1 Macc 2:7, 13 are also classifiable as non-cultic cries of lament. Each takes the form of question. Each is introduced by למה or ἵνα τι; in each an individual speaker inquires about the meaning of his or her life in the face of overwhelming sorrow. W. Schottroff, Der altisraelitische Fluchspruch WMANT 30 (Neukirchen-

framing words, ימי (18c) and היום (14a), and by the narrowness of its content which is concerned entirely with the matter of the curse.

Following Baumgartner,[40] some scholars have described the passage as a self-curse. However, attention to the close relationship between the compound curse and the cry of lament shows this to be an imprecise and misleading designation. The purpose of Jeremiah's curse is not to curse himself, nor God as some others propose.[41] It is to curse the day of his birth (v 14) and its attendant circumstances (vv 15-17). But the motivation for the curse presented in the climaxing cry of lament (v 18) does not derive from the birth itself. It comes from the unique misery of Jeremiah's life, a life of trouble and grief, which promise an equally dismal future.

A similar use of the birth motif appears in the second confession (15:10) where Jeremiah also laments his birth, not for its own sake but for the conflicts of his later life. (See Chapter 2.) This diversion of attention from the birth to the problem of Jeremiah's wearisome life indicates that the real issue in these two texts is not Jeremiah's birth but his life. The birth motif must be interpreted symbolically.[42] This is confirmed by the thematic and linguistic affinities of 20:14-18 with the account of Jeremiah's prophetic commission in c 1. In that account, Jeremiah was appointed a prophet before his birth (v 5). The pre-natal timing of his appointment suggests that the whole purpose of Jeremiah's birth, indeed, the reason he went forth from the womb, תצא מרחב, (1:5; cf., 20:18)[43] was to serve as a prophet to the nations.

Similarly, in the cursing poem of c 20 the birth motif functions as a symbol of Jeremiah's prophetic mission. The designation of this poem as a curse of his prophetic vocation bears some importance for the poem's interpretation. The relationship of the compound curse (vv 14-17) to the cry of lament (v 18) supports this view of the poem. V 18 laments the source of his grief—his woeful life as a prophet.

In an assessment of the language of v 18 combined with a form-critical judgment regarding the function of the whole passage, Clines and Gunn

---

Vluyn: Neukirchener, 1969) 76-78; Claus Westermann, *Forschung am Alten Testament*, TBu 24 (München: Chr. Kaiser, 1964) 292-294.

[40]Baumgartner, *Die Klagegedichte*, 67.

[41]Graf, *Das Buch*, 282.

[42]See Duhm's rejection of this passage as a result of his attempt to read it literally, *Das Buch*, 167.

[43]So correctly, Berridge, *Prophet*, 38, n. 76.

interpret the cursing poem differently.[44] For them, the poem curses the awful judgment soon to come upon Israel. The poem has nothing to do with the prophet's struggle with his mission. Linguistically these two scholars contend that the words בשׁת (and בוש) and יגון, found in the climaxing verse of the poem, refer only to the external conditions connected with the fate of the people. They exclude any subjective experience of the prophet from the poem.

It is true that the first word they examine, בשׁת (Jer 2:26), refers to the external, objective shame which falls upon Israel. But in the very same verse the shame of the people is made analogous to the individual shame which overwhelms the thief caught in crime. One wonders what criterion excludes subjective and individual nuances from the word's sphere of meaning. Similarly, when the people who have been sinning say "Let us lie down in our shame" (13:25), or, when Yahweh asks "Is it I whom they provoke? . . . Is it not themselves to their own shame?" no criterion suggests itself to permit a clear distinction between subjective and objective, individual and corporate, components of shame.

The word בוש also appears endowed with a broad range of meanings. The mother of seven is shamed (15:9); the farmers are ashamed of their harvest (14:4); Jeremiah asks not to be put to shame (17:18). In addition to the objective meanings mentioned by Clines and Gunn, each of the above occurrences incorporates a nuance of individual and subjective humiliation which has little or nothing to do with the fate of the people. Furthermore, the authors' contention that יגון refers exclusively to Jeremiah's sorrow over the approaching fate of Judah cannot be sustained because it fails to note one important occurrence of the noun. In 45:3 Baruch laments his own sorrow and pain in clearly personal terms. Yahweh replies to his complaint. "Do you seek great things for yourself?" (45:5) Yahweh distinguishes Baruch's fate from the doom awaiting "all flesh." "I will give your life as a prize of war." (45:5) It cannot be argued on the basis of the language of v 18, therefore, that the poem excludes expressions of the prophet's own sorrow. Nor can it be said that the chief concern of the poem is the fate of the people.

On the other hand, support for the argument that the poem curses the personal circumstances of Jeremiah's life can be drawn from the parallel passage traditionally cited in connection with Jer 20:14-18, the long cursing poem of Job 3:3-26. Though literary dependence between these two

---

[44]Clines and Gunn, "Form, Occasion and Redaction," 405-407. The form-critical argument will be treated below.

passages cannot be established in either direction,[45] these two texts exhibit abundant formal and material parallels. The content of the verses from the Job passage corresponds closely to verses of the Jeremiah poem:

Jb	3:3a	Jer	20:14
	3b		15
	5,8		16
	10		17
	11		18[46]

Furthermore, the Job poem contains variations of the same form-critical elements found in Jeremiah's poem, a curse of the day of his birth and connected circumstances (3-10), followed by compound cries of lament which question the meaning of Job's existence (11-19). The literary purpose of the sage's poem can hardly be disputed—to express Job's dismay as he confronts the singular misery of his life. By analogy to the Job text, therefore, Jeremiah's poem also expresses his grief about the unique tribulation of his life, namely, the tribulation brought upon him by his prophetic mission.

The conclusion that the poem of Jer 20:14-18 is a curse of Jeremiah's prophetic mission prompts efforts to locate this curse within the context of the prophet's own life. On form-critical grounds joined with their linguistic arguments presented above, Clines and Gunn maintain that the poem functions in a manner similar to the literary form identified by D. Hillers, the response to bad news.[47]

Though that form is cast in language expressive of subjective grief, its exclusive function is to emphasize the awful content of the message received, not the subjective response to the message by its recipients. Clines and Gunn, therefore, understand Jeremiah's poem as a commentary upon the content of his own message: it is bad news.

In response to this argument it need only be pointed out, as the authors themselves admit, that the conventional form is completely absent from the poem. Indeed, the only point of comparison between the Jer 20:14-18

---

[45]G. Fohrer, *Das Buch Hiob* KAT 16; (Gütersloh: Gütersloher Verlagshaus Gerd Mohn, 1963) 113; F. Horst, *Hiob* BKAT 16/1 (Neukirchen-Vluyn: Neukirchener Verlag, 1968) 41.

[46]Artur Weiser, *Das Buch Hiob* ATD 13 (Göttingen: Vandenhoeck & Ruprecht, 1957) 38-40.

[47]Delbert Hillers, "A Convention in Hebrew Literature: The Reaction to Bad News," *ZAW* 77 (1965) 86-89.

and the conventional form is that there is news involved. In Jeremiah's curse the news is good news, at least for its recipient if not ultimately for Jeremiah himself. The comparison of 20:14-18 with the response to bad news form does not yield a solid basis for determining the original occasion which may have given rise to the poem.

Perhaps a better clue, though admittedly only a clue, can be found by comparing Jer 20:14-18 with a verse of the second confession, 15:10. This verse is a lament of Jeremiah's prophetic mission expressed through the symbolic birth motif. In his analysis of this confession, F. Hubmann[48] proposes that a key for understanding 15:10 can be located in the expression איש ריב איש מדון. When the two words, מדון and ריב, appear together the latter term loses its legal connotations so that both terms function as synonyms for human conflict or disagreement.[49] In 15:10, therefore, when Jeremiah laments his birth because he is איש ריב איש מדון, Hubmann proposes that Jeremiah is complaining about the human conflict his prophetic mission causes in the land. The nature of this human conflict may, in turn, be understood by noting the second sentence of this same verse. Here it is said that Jeremiah neither lends nor borrows, yet he is cursed by "all of them." In this notoriously difficult line, it is not failure to engage in mercenary activities which evokes the bitter response from his enemies, argues Hubmann. Jeremiah's failure to borrow or lend prophetic material among the community of prophets is the cause of his troubles. The human strife and contention lamented by Jeremiah in 15:10, therefore, may refer to the discord caused by the independence of his prophetic message from that of the circle of prophets.[50]

Though this is an original and interesting interpretation, the phrase is probably a simple wisdom expression through which Jeremiah complains that he is despised despite his good behavior.[51] (See Chapter 2.) Though it is difficult to decide the exact meaning of the phrase, it is clear that Jeremiah's life involves conflicts with his enemies.

In Jer 20:14-18, the presence of the same motifs as in 15:10, the cursing of his birth and the tribulation caused by his prophetic ministry, argue that the poem's setting may be Jeremiah's conflict with the false prophets. This proposal gains credibility from the poem's redactional

---

[48]Hubmann, *Untersuchungen*, 259-260.

[49]Cf., Prov 15:18; 17:14 and 22:10 where מדון is used with איש supporting Hubmann's assertion.

[50]Cf., 23:30 where a related idea is expressed in what is probably Deuteronomistic language.

[51]Cf., Pro 22:7.

placement next to the confession of praise (20:7-13). These two pieces share themes of anguish and lamentation and both may arise from Jeremiah's conflict with the false prophets. (See Chapter 6.) However, these pieces of evidence are, at best, only suggestive. As a consequence, this attempt to reconstruct an original setting for the cursing poem in the life of the prophet must remain in the realm of hypothesis. What is certain is that the piece is not part of the fifth confession. The redactional function of the cursing poem is considered in Chapter 8.

6

The Confessions as a Collection of Poems

I. THE SCHOLARLY DEBATE

Characterized by the expression of intensely personal feelings, almost modern in their apparent introspection, the confessions of Jeremiah (11:18-12:6; 15:10-21; 17:14-18; 18:18-23; 20:7-13[1]), are unique among prophetic writings. In view of this singularity of content, it is surprising that scholars have reached little consensus in their interpretation. Agreement appears to be limited to two general conclusions. Most scholars assume that Jeremiah's confessions circulated as an independent collection before being incorporated into the larger Jeremianic compilation.[2] And, since the publication of W. Baumgartner's form-critical analysis of the confessions, *Die Klagegedichte des Jeremia*,[3] no one has seriously contested the conclusion that all the confessions employ some elements of the psalm of lament form.

Beyond this limited consensus in their interpretation the unusualness of the content of the confessions has given rise to a series of interrelated problems for which few satisfactory solutions have been proposed. There is, first, the difficulty of establishing the original purpose of their composition and, associated with this question, there is the problem of identifying the speaker, "*das Ich*," of the poems. Then there is the matter of providing the collectors with a reason for preserving the peoms, which

---

[1]20:14-18, considered part of the fifth confession by many interpreters, is more properly classified as a cursing poem placed after the fifth confession for redactional purposes. See Chapter 5.

[2]Cf. Von Rad, "Die Konfessionen," and *Old Testament Theology*, II, D. M. G. Stalker, trans. (New York: Harper & Row, 1965) 204; Bright, AB, LXVI; Ittmann, *Die Konfessionen*, 187-192.

[3]BZAW 32 (Giessen: A. Töpelmann, 1917).

appear to have a biographical rather than a prophetic significance. Finally, there is the difficulty of discerning whether the confessions can be interpreted as a unit, or whether they should be approached, instead, as isolated poetic pieces. Scholarly efforts to solve these puzzles can be divided into three distinct points of view.

Perhaps the most widely accepted set of solutions to these problems of interpretation has been advanced by John Bright.[4] According to this classic view, the confessions express Jeremiah's personal cries of distress, each arising from separate historical events of the prophet's difficult life. And, while the occasions of their composition do not admit of firm historical reconstruction, there is sufficient knowledge of the prophet's circumstances available to provide a general context for the confessions' production.[5] The personal voice of the historical Jeremiah, therefore, stands behind the "I" of these laments which served as private poems of distress, not public prophetic oracles.[6] Motivation for the preservation and collection of the confessions, in this view, derives from biographical interest in the man Jeremiah whose psychological turmoil bespeaks the common human struggle. Since, in Bright's opinion, each of these five pieces is understood to have arisen from a discrete historical moment in Jeremiah's life, the relationship of the confessions to one another is seen to rest exclusively in their expression of similar context and in their participation in a common literary genre.

Although their works differ on some essential points, the studies of Reventlow, Gunneweg and Gerstenberger represent the other end of the interpretive spectrum.[7] In contrast to Bright's position, all three of these

---

[4]AB; "Jeremiah's Complaints: Liturgy or Expressions of Personal Distress?" in *Proclamation and Presence: Old Testament Essays in Honour of G. H. Davies,* J. I. Durham, and J. R. Porter, eds. (London: SCM Press, 1970) 189-214; and "A Prophet's Lament."

[5]For example, see AB, 112. Such also is the view of J. Skinner, *Prophecy and Religion.*

[6]AB, LXVI.

[7]H. Graf Reventlow, *Liturgie und prophetisches Ich bei Jeremia,* (Gütersloh: Gerd Mohn, 1963); A. H. J. Gunneweg, "Konfession oder Interpretation im Jeremiabuch," *ZTK* 67/4 (1970) 395-416; Erhard Gerstenberger, "Jeremiah's Complaints: Observations on Jer. 15:10-21," *JBL* 82/4 (1963) 393-408. See also Carroll, *From Chaos to Cov,* 107-135, who follows and amplifies Gerstenberger's view that the confessions have been arranged redactionally to present Jeremiah as typical of Israel, but also as a rejected prophet. His thesis rests on the similarities among the confessions, the Psalms and Job. These similarities strongly suggest to

scholars agree that the confessions contain no information regarding the interior, emotional life of the prophet. The "I" of the poems should be understood as the corporate "I" of the psalms, that is, as a typical or literary "I," whether as the device of the prophet (Reventlow), or as the fiction of later editors (Gunneweg and Gerstenberger). Rather than having been preserved by the force of biographical interest in Jeremiah, these pieces found a place in the prophetic corpus because their function was a purely public one—to announce the prophetic word to the community. Building upon the fundamental presupposition that the primary role of the prophet was that of cultic mediator, Reventlow claims that the confessions are psalms of lamentation of the community, not of the individual. Their public function was to express the community's response to God's word of judgment. Reventlow's position has been successfully refuted by a number of scholars and need not be developed here.[8]

Gunneweg's contribution to this discussion is his demonstration that the confession of c 15 employs the psalm of individual lament form. But for Gunneweg, this form is viewed as a literary device of a later editor who juxtaposes biographical data drawn from Jeremianic traditions with the features of the individual lament. This editor represented Jeremiah as a typical figure of the righteous sufferer who experiences the fate of all Israel.[9]

The scholarly positions so far presented in this study interpret the confessions from a one-dimensional perspective, viewing them either as entirely subjective or entirely objective in their content and function. Gerhard von Rad's work offers a more nuanced position which stands between these two extreme interpretations.[10] For von Rad, the subjective elements of the confessions are undeniable. These poems are expressions of personal anger and distress. Unlike other prophetic materials they are not commissioned announcements to Israel. They are personal complaints addressed to God. "Die Richtung seiner Worte geht nicht von oben nach

---

Carroll that Jeremiah is not their author. Such a position, however, ignores the presence of complaints and laments found elsewhere within the poetic material of Jeremiah.

[8]See, for instance, J. M. Berridge, *Prophet*; Bright, "Jeremiah's Complaints"; and Gunneweg "Konfession."

[9]Gunneweg, "Konfession."

[10]"Die Konfessionen Jeremias," *EvT* 3 (1936), 265-276. See also *The Message of the Prophets*, D. M. G. Stalker, trans. (New York: Harper & Row, 1967) 170-175.

unten, sondern von unten nach oben. . . ."[11] For von Rad, such an encroachment of the subjective into prophetic literature marks the disintegration of classical prophecy.

But in his view the confessions also bear a prophetic stamp. When Jeremiah spoke as an individual, he also spoke as a prophet. Thus his personal words also function prophetically. They introduce a new conception of the prophetic office in which the suffering man and the prophet are united so that the prophet witnesses to God even in his broken humanity. For von Rad, Jeremiah's brokenness revealed in the confessions also expresses the need for healing of all the people of Israel. At the same time, the confessions testify to the austerity of God's anger against this people.

The result of this view is that, on one level, the "I" of the confessions is the personal voice of the man Jeremiah and, on a second, symbolic level, the "I" acquires the added voice of the community of Israel. The prophet and the community receive only a silent response from an angry God. Such a perception of the dual function of the confessions provides a reasonable explanation for their preservation and collection. The community was interested in these pieces because they functioned, at least secondarily, as prophetic material.

An important contribution of von Rad to the study of the confessions has been his proposal that the five confessions should be approached as a unified collection of poetry. He claims that the order of their placement within the Biblical text exhibits a development of thought or argument. The basis for this judgment is two-fold. First, the two initial confessions contain oracles of assurance from Yahweh (12:5-6 and 15:19-21), creating a dialogue between Yahweh and the prophet. The disappearance of these oracles in the latter three confessions is evidence for von Rad that Jeremiah has been left alone to recite despairing soliloquies. Second, the anger and bitterness of the last confession (20:7-18), seals Jeremiah's entry into a mood of total abandonment in his prophetic task. Consequently in von Rad's approach the confessions descend toward an abyss of greater and greater darkness and despair.

Drawing upon the results of the previous five chapters, the present chapter addresses these unresolved questions in the interpretation of the confessions. It agrees with von Rad's judgment that the confessions played both a private and a public role during Jeremiah's lifetime, but it offers a different view of the nature and importance of their public function. The argument of this chapter is drawn from a consideration of the purpose of

---

[11]"Die Konfessionen," 267.

the individual confessions which has been demonstrated in each of the preceding chapters. It considers the content and language of the confessions particularly from the perspective that these pieces can be understood as a collection of poems. From this synthesis, it draws further conclusions regarding the identity of the speaker and regarding the reasons for the preservation and the collection of the poems. Finally, it utilizes arguments derived from the content and literary form of the confessions to propose an alternative to von Rad's view of the development of thought within the collection.

II. THE PURPOSE OF THE CONFESSIONS

The exegetical analysis of the individual confessions has shown that the primary purpose of each confession was to establish the authenticity of Jeremiah's claim to be the true prophet of Yahweh. Each aspect of the content of these poems adds strength to this claim and serves to distinguish Jeremiah sharply from the false prophets. The false prophets were legion during his time and posed a profound threat to Israel's acceptance of the word of Yahweh.[12] An attempt is made in this chapter to synthesize those aspects of the confessions which form Jeremiah's argument for the legitimacy of his avowed role. This synthesis is intended to serve as the foundation for solutions to the unresolved questions raised above.

A. Content of the Confessions

Jeremiah's arguments in the confessions that he is a true prophet fall into three major categories. The first category presents Jeremiah as a prophet faithful to his task. The second presents Yahweh as the controlling power and originator of the prophet's work. The last category comprises Yahweh's two responses to Jeremiah's complaints.

---

[12]Cf., 2:8, 26, 30; 5:30-31; 8:10; 14:13-16, 18; 23:9-40; 28; 29:24-32. The problem of false prophecy shows up in all the Jeremianic sources leaving little doubt that this phenomenon created a major problem for Jeremiah's life. See I. Meyer, *Jeremia und die Falschen Propheten*, Orbis Biblicus et Orientalis 13 (Göttingen: Vandenhoeck and Ruprecht, 1977) and I. Meyer and F. L. Hossfeld, *Prophet Gegen Prophet: Eine Analyse des alttestamentlichen Texte zum Thema: wahre und falsche Propheten*, BB 9 (Fribourg: Schweizerisches Katholisches Bibelwerk, 1973).

1. Jeremiah as Faithful

a. Jeremiah depicts himself as innocent of all wrongdoing and faithful to his role as mediator between Yahweh and Israel. He is a lamb led to the slaughter (11:19), righteous before Yahweh (12:3 and see 15:10cd). He devoured and delighted in Yahweh's words (15:16). He reminds Yahweh of how he interceded for the people (18:20).

b. Jeremiah professes a special relationship with Yahweh. Yahweh caused him to know the deeds of his enemies (11:18). Jeremiah is with Yahweh (12:3) and called by Yahweh's name (15:16). Yahweh is his refuge (17:17) and present to him as a mighty warrior (20:11).

The significance of these two assertions for Jeremiah's larger claim to be a true spokesman for Yahweh becomes evident in light of the indictment against false prophets found in 23:18-22. In contrast to Jeremiah, the false prophets of this poem are evil and they refuse to turn from their evil ways (v 22). Nor do they have any relationship with Yahweh, having neither stood in his council nor listened to his word (v 18). Jeremiah alone holds these distinctions and they qualify him as a prophet.

2. Yahweh as Originator

Most of the attention in the confessions is directed to Yahweh. It is God who must take the blame and responsibility for Jeremiah's predicament.

a. Yahweh is depicted as overpowering the prophet. Jeremiah sat alone because Yahweh's hand was upon him (15:17). Yahweh deceived him and overpowered him (20:7), and when Jeremiah tries to evade his prophetic duty, he was overpowered by the fire in his being (20:7).

b. Jeremiah asserts without any qualification that the message he was compelled to speak was not his own but Yahweh's (15:16ab). Yahweh filled him with indignation, with the evil message (15:17), and Yahweh witnessed all that Jeremiah proclaimed (17:16). It is the word of God which caused all the prophet's sufferings (20:8).

c. Yahweh is the one accused in the confessions. The Righteous Judge causes the wicked to flourish and brings evil upon the land (12:1-4). God is a deceitful spring not to be trusted (15:18) and God is the one who seduces and overpowers the prophet (20:7).

By means of these three arguments, Jeremiah further separates himself from the false prophets. The false prophets "ran" to prophesy on their own initiative (23:21), and they spoke without hearing Yahweh's word or standing in his heavenly council to receive his message.[13] Not so, Jeremiah. He did not wish to prophesy; he was compelled to prophesy by the irresistible power of Yahweh. And he did not invent his prophetic message; he wanted nothing whatsoever to do with it.

Above all, therefore, the confessions express Jeremiah's mighty resistance to the prophetic mission. The purpose of these expressions of resistance was to counter the accusation that his prophecy was false. For this reason, Jeremiah accuses Yahweh of treachery and infidelity in relation to his prophet. All Jeremiah's prophetic activity and all its consequences for him of suffering and persecution are blamed upon Yahweh to show that Jeremiah was helpless in the face of Yahweh's domineering power.[14]

3. Yahweh's Replies

The responses of Yahweh to the prophet's complaints in the first two confessions are important because they reveal what Yahweh expects of a true prophet. The genuine prophet must anticipate suffering and mounting persecution (12:5 and the redactional v 6 which expands this idea), and a true prophet must meet certain conditions or behavioral expectations

---

[13]23:18, 21-22; cf., 1 Kgs 22. This same anti-prophetic polemic also shows up in the prose passage 14:14. Although Jeremiah's enemies remain, for the most part, colorless and anonymous throughout the Book (11:19; 18:18-23; 17:8, 15; 6:10), the opponents clearly aim their attack at the authenticity of Jeremiah's message. They refuse to listen to his word (6:10); they attempt to discredit his prophecy (6:10; 18:18); they doubt the truth of his message because it has failed the Deuteronomistic test for true prophecy—fulfillment (17:15; Dt 18:22, cf., Jer 28:9). Jeremiah's enemies may not be prophets, but they wish to identify Jeremiah as a false prophet. For scholarly discussion of false prophecy, see especially J. L. Crenshaw, *Prophetic Conflict: Its Effects upon Israelite Religion*, BZAW 125 (Berlin: Walter de Gruyter, 1971); Eva Oswald, *Falsche Prophetie im Alten Testament*, SGVGGTR 237 (Tübingen: J. C. B. Mohr, 1962); and Hossfeld and Meyer, *Prophet Gegen Prophet*; and Robert P. Carroll, *When Prophecy Failed: Cognitive Dissonance in the Prophetic Traditions of the Old Testament* (New York: Seabury, 1979).

[14]The same compulsion-resistance themes appear in the call narrative which is closely linked to the confessions in language and purpose. See Chapter 7.

(15:19). Unlike the false prophets who refuse to turn (שוב) from their evil
ways (23:22), the authentic spokesman must turn (שוב) to Yahweh (15:19).
The false prophets delivered their own lying message (23:21), but the true
prophet must speak what is pure and precious (15:19). These responses of
Yahweh, therefore, are genuine oracles of assurance to Jeremiah because
they accord precisely with Jeremiah's situation and with his own claims in
the other arguments of the confessions. Furthermore, these oracles serve
as public, divine seals of approval upon the prophet who is refused a hearing by his stubborn people.

B. Rîb Language of the Confessions

The thesis that the original purpose of the Jeremianic confessions was
to legitimate Jeremiah as a true prophet, receives added support from
another aspect of the content of the confessions. The entire collection of
poems uses the conventional language of the rîb or covenant lawsuit
motif. W. Holladay[15] has discussed the importance of the lawsuit in the
confessions and sees in it an explanation of Jeremiah's accusations against
Yahweh. In Holladay's view, the rîb was employed to give legal definition
to Jeremiah's faltering relationship with Yahweh. The need to clarify the
relationship gave rise to Jeremiah's rîb or complaint against Yahweh.

Holladay's argument, however, puts the pieces of the argument in
reverse order. The challenge does not arise from the lawsuit motif but
from the purpose of the confessions themselves—to vindicate Jeremiah as
Yahweh's true spokesman. The rîb motif provides the linguistic and conceptual framework for this argument which includes accusations against
Yahweh. Rather than explaining the presence of theodicy in the confessions, as Holladay proposes, the rîb is a tool employed to give shape and
texture to the argument of legitimation.

The first thing to be noted about the rîb motif in the confessions is that
the collection of five poems is framed by a so-called doublet (11:20 and
20:12), which presents Jeremiah's rîb petition to Yahweh.[16] Because most
scholars have included 20:14-18 as part of the fifth confession, this
literary enclosure has gone unnoticed. In this study 20:14-18 has been

---

[15]"Jeremiah's Lawsuit with God, A Study in Suffering and Meaning," *Int*
17 (1963) 280-287.
[16]See Chapter 5 for a discussion of the similarities and differences
between the two verses and for the reasons for retaining both verses.
Note that the confessions do not employ the literary genre of the rîb but
only its language.

disqualified both as an element of the fifth confession and as a separate
confession in itself. The pericope does not conform to the form-critical
features of the psalm of individual lament as do all the other confessions,
but, with Job 3, includes appropriate elements to classify it as a cursing
poem, placed after the confession for redactional purposes.[17]

This form-critical decision means that the second last verse of the fifth
confession (20:12),

ויהוה בחן צדיק ראה כליות ולב
אראה נקמתך מהם כי אליך גליתי את ריבי

creates a literary frame with the third verse of the first confession
(11:20),

ויהוה שפט צדק בחן כליות ולב
אראה נקמתך מהם כי אליך גליתי את-ריבי.

Though the framing doublet does not prove literary intentionality, its
presence strengthens the hypothesis that the confessions once circulated
as an independent collection of poems. Moreover, the verse's repetition
promises that these poems may be interpreted as a collection of poetry
rather than only as independent units. If so, the literary enclosure of 11:20
and 20:12 establishes the conceptual framework within which Jeremiah
makes his claim for authenticity as a true prophet. The correctness of this
position becomes evident when attention is paid to the conventional covenant lawsuit language found not only in the doublet but throughout the
confessions.

In the doublet Jeremiah's request for vindication includes an assertion
that Yahweh is a Righteous Judge[18] who tests minds and hearts and,
second, a motive (כי) for Yahweh to meet the request, "for to you I have
revealed my complaint." This motive clause suggests that merely to

---

[17]Cf., Holladay, *Architecture*, 136, on echoes of 1:5.

[18]In *rîb* texts Yahweh is frequently declared righteous as judge, Dt
32:4; 2 Chron 12:6; Ps 50:6; Mich 6:5. Cf. Julien Harvey, *Le Plaidoyer prophétique contre Israël après la rupture de l'alliance: Etude d'une formula
litteraire L'Ancien Testament*, Studia 22 (Paris: Desclee de Brouwer,
1967) 109. See Jeremiah's play on this motif in 12:1-3.

reveal the *rîb*[19] to the Righteous Judge will cause Yahweh to intervene. The doublet carries with it, therefore, implicit confidence in the justice of Yahweh and in Yahweh's partiality to Jeremiah's *rîb*.

In 11:20 Jeremiah's complaint is leveled against his enemies, but in 12:1-4 his complaint is lodged directly against the Just Judge. In this instance, the Judge is accused of failing to do justice. The wicked prevail while the Judge is implicated in fostering their growth. Thus Jeremiah plays with the *rîb* motif to strengthen his argument that Yahweh is in control of the prophet's whole existence.

In 15:10 Jeremiah describes himself as an איש ריב, that is, one whose role is legal adversary to the whole land.[20] In 18:19 Jeremiah again appeals to Yahweh to hear his complaint (ושמע לקל ריבי)[21], with the implicit assumption that if Yahweh will listen carefully, action will surely follow. Consequently, the *rîb* is mentioned explicitly in four of the five confessions, setting Jeremiah against the enemies who refuse to hear his word and against Yahweh who fails to fulfill that word.

In addition to the explicit mention of the *rîb* motif, the confessions prominently feature the word ידע, also commonly found in Ancient Near Eastern covenant texts. In these texts ידע means legal recognition between covenant partners or recognition of treaty stipulations which are binding.[22] This background illuminates Jeremiah's use of the term in the confessions.

The term ידע occurs four times[23] in the confessions and in each instance it adds weight to Jeremiah's claim that he is a true prophet. In

---

[19]See James Limbourg, "The Root ריב and the Prophetic Lawsuit Speeches," *JBL* 88 (1969) 291-304, for a discussion of the primary meanings of this root.

[20]See Limbourg, *Jeremiah*, 298.

[21]The term שמע is ubiquitous in *rîb* texts (see Harvey, *Le Plaidoyer prophétique*, 107). See also its use in 18:22 where Jeremiah uses the passive form to propose a dreadful fate for the enemy. Their distress will "be heard."

[22]See Delbert Hillers, *Covenant: The History of a Biblical Idea* (Baltimore: Johns Hopkins, 1969) 120; and Herbert Huffmon, "The Covenant Lawsuit in the Prophets," *JBL* 78 (1959) 285-295, and "The Treaty Background of YADA," *BASOR* 181 (1966) 31-37.

[23]The 11:18 usage, a fifth occurrence, is difficult to interpret precisely. The "causing to know" seems to involve a prior revelation to Jeremiah regarding the evil schemes of his enemies and, therefore, may not carry any covenantal nuances. It does indicate, though, that Jeremiah claims a special relationship with Yahweh.

12:3, Jeremiah asserts that Yahweh knows him, tests him and finds him loyal. In the context of the *rîb* such language claims for Jeremiah a mutually loyal covenant relationship with Yahweh. The second confession (15:15; see Text Critical Note) combines ידע with another conventional covenant term,[24] זכר. In covenant contexts the defendant often recalls past events to support or defend his position against accusation.[25] Here Jeremiah calls upon Yahweh to recognize and remember the past relationship between them as a basis for the prophet's request for vengeance.

The last two uses of the term, זכר, (17:16 and 18:23) assert that Yahweh is the legal witness, in the first instance, to all Jeremiah's prophecies, and in the second, to the plots of his wicked enemies. Since Yahweh recognizes both the truth of Jeremiah's prophecy and the evil of his enemies' deeds, these assertions become the basis for Jeremiah's further requests for vengeance. All four of these occurrences of זכר also employ the second singular personal pronoun (אתה) with the name of Yahweh. Such a full form of address emphasizes Yahweh's responsibility in the act of legally recognizing the prophet.

The covenant *rîb* language in the confessions, therefore, functions as a vehicle to support Jeremiah's main argument. First, the framing of the confessions by the doublet sets all the poems within the boundaries of a subtle assertion that Yahweh is Just Judge who will hear and act on behalf of the prophet. Second, the *rîb* language sets Jeremiah against the enemies who refuse to hear the word (11:20; 15:10; 20:12), and at the same time, provides Jeremiah with language to blame Yahweh for his predicament (12:1-3). This results in absolving Jeremiah from responsibility for the nature and effects of his prophecy. Third, the utilization of ידע allows Jeremiah to strengthen his claim that he exists in a special relationship with Yahweh who will ultimately vindicate him.

This consideration of the content of the confessions viewed as a collection of poems has shown that the original purpose of Jeremiah's confessions was to claim for Jeremiah the role of authentic spokesman for Yahweh. This means that the confessions had an intrinsic public function in the lifetime of the prophet. If this thesis is correct, a number of conclusions follow for the interpretation of the confessions.

The subjective, personal aspects of the confession operate in the

---

[24]See Harvey, *Le Plaidoyer prophétique*, 108-109, and B. Childs, *Memory and Tradition in Israel*, SBT 37 (London: SCM Press, 1962) 48-49; and Limbourg, *Jeremiah*, 30.

[25]Cf. Childs, *Memory*, 48-49.

cleverest way possible to defend Jeremiah from association with the false prophets. The subjectivity, therefore, has a clear public purpose. This does not mean that the personal content of these poems needs to be viewed as a useful fiction, but it does mean that the subjective aspects have much more than a purely psychological or biographical value.[26]

The "I" of these poems must be understood as the personal voice of Jeremiah and can in no way be interpreted to represent the voice of the community. The referent of the "I" is the specific person of the prophet, who, in no sense, stands for the people in the confessions. On the contrary, the speaker in the confessions stands over against the community as its adversary and prosecutor (איש ריב). And, although he intercedes on behalf of the community (18:20), he alone acts in the unique role of spokesman for Yahweh, a role that was hardly the activity of the community during Jeremiah's time nor immediately afterwards. The community resists completely the speaker in these confessions. If there is any symbolic identification of the "I" of the confessions with the people of Israel, it is not to be found on the level of the confessions' original purpose.

The motivation for the preservation and collection of the confessions would not be limited to a biographical interest in the man Jeremiah. No other piece of prophetic writing has been preserved for such a reason and neither are these. The confessions were preserved because they claimed that Jeremiah's prophecy was true and they appealed to God's authority for that truth. The confessions were prophetic. And, to a later generation who found that Jeremiah was vindicated and his prophecy fulfilled, these poems would supply further evidence of the hardness of Israel's heart and of the refusal of the people to listen to the prophet like Moses.

---

[26]As Crenshaw has remarked in a discussion of pathos in the Wisdom literature, "The Human Dilemma and the Literature of Dissent," *Tradition and Theology in the Old Testament*, Douglas Knight, ed. (Philadelphia: Fortress, 1977) 236-237, "Use of traditional . . . genre does not indicate any lack of personal sincerity." Similarly, there is no reason to deny that Jeremiah's employment of the conventional genre of the psalm of individual lament expressed his personal struggle with his prophetic mission. Rather, it is to argue that the primary reason this expression of personal suffering was remembered and preserved is because of the public claim it made for Jeremiah's role as true prophet in the face of disbelieving and mocking opponents who tried to claim the same role for themselves and so placed the word of Yahweh itself in jeopardy.

III. THE RELATIONSHIP OF THE CONFESSIONS
TO ONE ANOTHER

The major evidence for von Rad's thesis that the confessions, when viewed as a collection, move toward a decrescendo of darkness has been construed differently in the previous sections of this paper. The oracles of assurance from Yahweh in the first two confessions have not been understood as evidence of a dialogue between Yahweh and the prophet which later ceased, but as divine certifications that Jeremiah would meet the expected conditions of true prophecy. And the fifth confession (20:7-13) has not been perceived as the nadir of Jeremiah's gloom because vv 14-18 have been eliminated from it. Rather than moving toward an abyss of despair for the prophet and for Israel, the confessions move in the opposite direction of von Rad's assessment—toward greater confidence that Yahweh will vindicate the prophet and fulfill the prophetic word. This movement toward light, assurance and praise is evident in the content of the confessions and in their form-critical components.

In the first two confessions (11:18-12:6 and 15:10-21), Jeremiah's complaints are bitter (11:18-19; 15:10-11), and his accusations against Yahweh are strident (12:1-4 and 15:18). In the third confession (17:14-18), the themes of anger and grief are softened and an element of confidence and praise enters the prophet's prayer. The pain and the wound which were declared endless, incurable and unable to be healed in 15:18 are submitted to Yahweh in 17:14. And Yahweh is no longer the "deceitful spring" in this confession, but the one who has the power to heal and to save. Yahweh is Jeremiah's refuge (17:17). Almost entirely petition, the fourth confession (18:18-23) is devoted to requests that disaster will befall the enemies, that is, that the prophetic judgment Jeremiah has been proclaiming will be fulfilled.

While the complaint of the fifth confession (20:7-13) appears at first to express the deepest despair and helplessness at the hands of an overpowering and deceptive God, these themes have already been shown to function as authorizations of Jeremiah's authenticity as a prophet. This confession, moreover, does not end with the complaint but goes on to assert the utmost confidence in Yahweh's saving power. It celebrates God's victory over the enemies as if this triumph had already occurred. "Yahweh is with me as a mighty Warrior." My pursuers will be destroyed. Yahweh is the judge of the righteous who will vindicate Jeremiah because Yahweh has heard his *rîb*. Therefore, "sing to Yahweh!" Such are the expressions of a prophet with full trust and confidence in a sovereign God who will vindicate him.

The form-critical components of the confessions reveal a corresponding movement toward praise and confidence in Yahweh. All of the confessions can be classified as psalms of individual lament, but not all of them contain all the constitutive elements of that literary genre. The purpose of this literary form is to praise God with confidence and assurance in the midst of suffering through the four constitutive elements of complaint, petition, statement of confidence and call to praise. This study has already observed that the first two confessions lack the statement of confidence and the call to praise. It has also argued that Jeremiah was playing with and adapting the form to express the ambivalence of his position and to strengthen his indictment of Yahweh. He complained that he was a faithful, innocent prophet and he petitioned for God's intervention, but he refrained from explicit statements of confidence and praise to distance himself from Yahweh and so to underscore his accusations that his prophetic dilemma was Yahweh's responsibility.

Just as the content of the third confession softens the tone of attack upon Yahweh, so too, the literary components of the poem are expanded to include a statement of confidence within the opening petition (17:14) of that confession. The fourth confession again reduces the form to two features of complaint (18:20) and petition (18:19, 21-23), but the petition is the principal focus of this poem and the granting of the request is almost assumed throughout the piece.

The argument of the confessions reaches its fullest expression in the last confession (20:7-13) and in doing so it utilizes the full form of the psalm of individual lament: vv 7-10, complaint; v 11, statement of confidence; v 12, petition; v 13, call to praise. The movement of thought within this collection of prophetic prayers is, therefore, toward burgeoning confidence and hope that through Yahweh's intervention the prophet and the word will triumph.

Against the many commentators who find in the title "confessions" an infelicitous although traditional title,[27] these poems of Jeremiah are aptly named for they are confessions in the true sense. They confess Jeremiah's confident trust and praise for "Yahweh rescued the life of the needy from the hand of evildoers" (20:13).

---

[27]E.g., see Carroll, *From Chaos to Covenant*, 107.

IV. THE SETTING OF THE CONFESSIONS
IN THE PROPHET'S LIFE

The subtle nature of the confession's arguments for prophetic legitimation requires their original setting to be among the disciples of the prophet.[28] It would be they and not the general populace who would understand the prophet's claims of divine compulsion and human resistance, and it would be they who eagerly anticipated the fulfillment of the prophet's word.

Although the psalm of individual lament had an original *Sitz im Leben* in the cult, that genre was adapted to a variety of human situations outside the cultic setting such as the sickbed, places of isolation or battle.[29] It is not necessary, therefore, to understand the place of these psalms within the Temple. Indeed, their strident accusations against Yahweh make them improbable material for public worship. Moreover, Jeremiah's experience of rejection by many in the religious and political establishment indicate that his prophetic claims would not have been accepted there. The more likely arena for the recitation of the confessions would have been among those who supported him but who may have been losing faith in him due to his apparent failure.

That Jeremiah was surrounded by his own support group is indicated by the text itself. Baruch was his scribe and faithful companion.[30] The Shaphan family and some of the princes hid Jeremiah from Jehoiakim and generally protected him.[31] Moreover, Robert R. Wilson's study, *Prophecy and Society in Ancient Israel*,[32] has demonstrated that nearly all the prophets in Israel functioned within a circle of supporters who had certain

---

[28]So also Bright, AB LXVI.

[29]So Hermann Gunkel and Joachim Begrich, *Einleitung in die Psalmen*, HKAT (Göttingen: Vandenhoeck & Ruprecht, 1933) 165-172; and against Mowinckel, *The Psalms in Israel's Worship*, 2 vols., D. R. Ap-Thomas, trans., (Nashville: Abingdon, 1962) 37-39, 225 in I, and 1-20 in II, who saw the setting as exclusively cultic. But see Claus Westermann, *The Psalms: Structure, Content and Message* (Minneapolis: Augsburg: 1980) 55-56; and H. J. Kraus, *Psalmen*, BKAT XV/1 (Neukirchen-Vluyn: Neukirchener, 1960) XLX.

[30]Cf., cc 36 and 45.

[31]See Holladay, *Architecture*, 127, for a discussion of the relationships among these people. Cf., 26:24; 36:12; 36:25; 26:16.

[32](Philadelphia: Fortress, 1980).

traditional expectations of the prophet's behavior and language and, in turn, provided the prophet with a receptive audience.

This hypothesis gains credibility in light of Baruch's lament found in c 45. Though it differs from the confessions in its second hand narration by the prophet, this lament appears to be fashioned after Jeremiah's confessions. Baruch complains of sorrow added to pain caused by Yahweh. He uses psalmic language (יגוני, יגעתי, v 3, Pss 6:7; 69:4) and language which appears in the confessions (אוי-נא לי, cf., 15:10; אוי-לי, cf., 15:17). Like Jeremiah, he expresses his weariness (יגעתי, v 3, נלאיתי, 20:9). In addition, Yahweh's reply to Baruch follows the patterns of Yahweh's replies to the prophet found in the first two confessions (12:5 and 15:19). Baruch is told not to seek anything for himself, that he will escape only with his life. Like Jeremiah, he is rebuked. Finally, in the reply, Yahweh uses language found in the call narrative (45:4; cf., 1:10 and 15:20).

The presence of this lament suggests that Baruch might have been accustomed to hearing such poems recited by the prophet. If so, the genre used to legitimate the prophet in the midst of his supporters is also used by a disciple to confirm his role in preserving the prophecy of Jeremiah. This seems particularly likely since Baruch's lament is dated in the fourth year of Jehoiakim when the King destroyed the scroll and the prophet and his companion went into hiding.

7

The Contributions of the Confessions and Their Relationship to Their Immediate Contexts

I. THE PROBLEM

This study has argued that the confessions of Jeremiah existed originally as an independent collection of poems designed to gain Jeremiah acceptance as a true prophet among his supporters. If this perception is correct, a number of questions follow regarding their incorporation and positioning within the larger complex of Jeremianic traditions. Why were the confessions included in the Book at all if their original purpose was a private one? Does the inclusion of the confessions within the Book provide them with a new and different purpose? What principles, if any, operated in the assignment of the confessions to their specific locations in cc 11-20? Why were the confessions separated from one another rather than preserved as an homogenous unit as were, for example, the Oracles Concerning the Nations (cc 46-51)? Why were the confessions dispersed through such a limited portion of the text (cc 11-20) rather than throughout the Book? Lurking behind all these questions is, of course, the broader problem—are the confessions situated in cc 11-20 accidentally, or have they been placed there with deliberte literary purpose?

No scholarly investigations confront these matters head on. This state of affairs is due to the small number of studies devoted to the confessions and to the tendency of those few studies to treat the poems as isolated units.[1] The questions deriving from the literary context of the confessions

---

[1]For example, see Baumgartner, *Die Klagegedichte*; Von Rad, *Die Konfessionen*; Hubmann, *Untersuchung*; G. M. Behler, "Vocation nenacée et renouvelleé (Jer 15:10-11. 15-21)," *La Vie Spirituelle* 560 (1969) 539-67; and, more recently, Ittmann, *Die Konfessionen*. However, see Claus Westermann, *Jeremia* (Stuttgart: Calwer, 1967) 44-47, who sees the confessions related to their immediately preceding contexts as responses to

have been approached only indirectly in the discussions of the larger and, as yet, very entangled problem of the composition of the Book. This chapter now turns to the aspects of the larger discussion which relate to the location of the confessions within their immediate literary settings.

II. THE SCHOLARLY DISCUSSION: THE COMPOSITION OF THE BOOK AND THE LOCATION OF THE CONFESSION

Scholarly opinion regarding the process of the composition as it relates to the confessions can be divided into three broad, though overlapping, points of view. The first opinion, appearing in many of the older commentaries, maintains that the poetry in cc 1-25 is arranged chronologically, and hence, the confessions stand among the other materials in proper chronological order.[2] In such a view, the separation of the confessions is automatically understood as the result of lapses of time in their original recitation.

A second point of view, represented in the Weiser and Rudolph commentaries, also finds historical connection between the confessions and their contexts, but not necessarily a chronological one. Weiser proposes, for instance, that the first confession (11:18-12:6) was placed after an oracle critiquing the cult (11:15-17) because the confession depicts the anger of Jeremiah's priestly family at his attacks upon the cult.[3] Similarly, Rudolph suggests that the last confession,[4] was tied to the preceding prose narrative (20:1-6) because the editor possessed information connecting the confession to the prophet's altercation with Pashur.[5]

A third and more recent opinion holds that the technical procedures of oral transmission guided the arrangement of the materials. According to this argument, the confessions were attracted to their present positions by the operation of catchword and thematic mnemonic devices. For

---

commissions. (See below.) So also Ahuis, *Der Klagende*.

[2]Cf., Volz, *Der Prophet*, XXV; Leo Ad. Schneedorfer, *Das Buch Jeremiah: Des Propheten Klagelieder und Das Buch Baruch*, WKHSAT (Wien: von Mayer, 1903) XIX; Condamin, *Le Livre*, XXI-XXIV. Each of these commentaries supplies the reader with a chart organizing the poetry in precise chronological order.

[3]Weiser, *Das Buch*, 105.

[4]20:7-18 in his view but see Chapter 5.

[5]Rudolph, *Jeremia*, 128-129.

example, John Bright points to the presence of מגור מסביב (20:3 and 10), which links the last confession with the prose narrative,[6] and to the motif of the tree (11:16 and 19) which joins the first confession with the preceding pieces.[7] W. Holladay finds the materials in cc 11-20, including the confessions, to be organized around the catchwords אב and אם, the "father and mother complexes."[8]

None of these understandings of the composition of the Book answers the questions raised by the presence of the confessions in cc 11-20. The first two historically oriented theories are not satisfactory because evidence for anything more than a general dating of the material is absent from the text. Though scholars agree that the earlier chapters of the Book represent Jeremiah's earliest preaching, this assessment is based more upon the conciliatory nature of the material[9] than upon specific historical clues found in the text. As a result, the assignment of every oracle to the reign of a specific monarch, as is found in the elaborate chronological schemes of the earlier commentators, rests upon false methodological assumptions. The text simply does not permit such precise chronological judgments. One can simply observe the lack of unity among these chronological charts[10] to perceive the absence of uniform standards of judgment.

Scholarly attempts to provide the confessions with historical settings from juxtaposed materials in the text are no less speculative. The text provides only the fifth confession (20:7-13), and arguably the first (11:18-12:6), with an historical setting. The remaining three confessions are intermingled with miscellaneous materials[11] and, hence, are not accounted for by the argument. Furthermore, if the claims of the previous chapter are correct, the dating of the confessions cannot be gained from

---

[6]Bright, AB LXXV.

[7]Ibid., 88.

[8]See 12:6; 15:10 and 20:14-18. See also Holladay, *Architecture*, 128-129.

[9]See comments on structural arrangement in Chapter 8.

[10]Volz, *Der Prophet*, XXV; Condamin, *Le Livre*, XXII-XXIV; and Schneedorfer's discussion in *Das Buch*, XIX. See also Carroll's *From Chaos*, 5-30, for an extreme critique of efforts to reconstruct the historical Jeremiah from the text. Carroll's proposal argues that even Baruch was not an historical figure but a creation of the Deuteronomistic scribal school for the purposes of legitimating scribal influence over the Jeremianic traditions. But see footnote 12.

[11]For example, 17:14-18 follows wisdom sayings.

their context because they would have circulated independently of the prose and other poetic traditions. An editor may have been aware of historical connections among the tradition complexes, but such speculative historical links cannot be reconstructed. The prose traditions reveal that Jeremiah's life was continually threatened from 605 onward. The confessions may come from that year or from any time in his later ministry. The text provides neither criteria nor sufficient data for determining the precise historical incidents which precipitated them.[12]

Those who find superficial linguistic and thematic connections between some of the confessions and their contexts are surely correct, but they fail to provide a comprehensive explanation of the placement of the confessions in their contexts. The first difficulty is that few of the confessions exhibit catchword links with the surrounding materials.[13] The presence of repeated key words, moreover, admits of another

---

[12]Again see Carroll for an extremely negative assessment of the historicity of the Jeremianic traditions. For him, the scroll incident itself (c 26) is a fiction fashioned after the Josianic discovery of the scroll in the Temple. Such a pejorative view of the historical reliability of the prose materials solves some problems in the interpretation of the Book but it also raises many others. By ascribing enormous literary and theological creativity to the redactors, Carroll's view short-circuits the oral traditioning process and virtually severs the prophet from the later levels of the tradition. Carroll's proposal leads into the unsolved puzzle of the entire traditioning process—the tradition's creation, transmission and interpretation. As such, the dilemma extends far beyond the boundaries of this study.

In projecting such a sharp rupture between the life of the prophet and the creativity of the editors, however, Carroll's position appears untenable. Two arguments stand against it. First, recent linguistic studies point toward more continuity than discontinuity among the levels of the traditions. See Thomas W. Overholt, "Remarks on the Continuity of the Jeremiah Tradition," *JBL* 91 (1972) 457-462, and *Threat of Falsehood: A Study in the Theology in the Book of Jeremiah* SBT II, 16 (London: SCM Press, 1970); and J. M. Sturdy, "The Authorship of the 'Prose Sermons' of Jeremiah" in *Prophecy: Essays Presented to Georg Fohrer on his Sixty-fifth Birthday,* ed. by J. A. Emerton (Berlin: Walter de Gruyter, 1980) 143-150. Second, if one posits an Exilic date for the final redaction as Carroll does (although he leaves open the possibility of a post-Exilic date), then his alleged literary fictions could not have succeeded with Exiles who would have had memories of the actual events of the prophet's life.

[13]For example, 17:14-18 and 18:18-23 lack them or have only one. See below.

interpretation. They may not function as catchwords in the oral stages of transmission but, instead, be evidence of linguistic continuity between layers of the tradition.[14]

The second problem with the theories of assimilation during the oral transmission is that the confessions do not fit well topically with their surrounding materials: 11:18-12:6 adheres to its context only by virtue of its prose additions (11:21-31 and 12:6), while 17:14-18 exhibits no thematic links with its context. (See below.) A final flaw in this perception of the location of the confessions is that the principles of oral traditioning fail to explain why a tradent would have separated an originally homogenous collection of poetry rather than leave it intact like the Oracles Concerning the Nations (cc 46-51). A more comprehensive explanation of the confessions' location in cc 11-20 must be found.

To achieve a better understanding of the place of the confessions within the Book of Jeremiah the following procedures are used. First, to determine the purpose of their inclusion, the text is surveyed without the confessions. Next, to discover how they were wedded to the rest of the text, the confessions are studied in their immediate contexts. Finally, to assess why they were separated and placed only within cc 11-20, the confessions are scrutinized in light of the arrangement of materials in cc 1-25.

III. CHAPTERS 1-25 AND THE CONTRIBUTION OF THE CONFESSIONS

By eliminating the confessions from the Book, two thematic ingredients of cc 1-25 are either totally removed or sharply reduced. Without the confessions, virtually all evidence of Israel's persecution of the prophet, with one oblique exception, is removed from cc 1-19. Moreover, all requests of the prophet for vengeance upon his enemies are eradicated from the text. Each of these themes is considered below.

A. Rejection and Persecution of the Prophet

The poetic materials of cc 1-25 make occasional reference to the people's intransigence when confronted with Yahweh's word.

---

[14]See the works of Overholt and Sturdy cited in note 12 above.

> Hear this, O foolish and senseless people
> who have eyes, but see not
> who have ears, but hear not (5:21, RSV).

> Behold, their ears are closed, they cannot listen:
> Behold, the word of the Lord is an object of scorn to
> them, they take no pleasure in it (6:10, RSV).

> I set watchmen over you, saying,
> "Give heed to the sound of the trumpet."
> But they would not give heed (6:17, RSV).

Although these three passages pointedly accuse the people of rejecting Yahweh's word, nowhere in the poetry is there any indication that the people rejected or persecuted the prophet himself.

Similarly, within the prose materials of cc 1-25 there are denunciations of Israel for refusing to listen to Yahweh's word. When Yahweh called to them (7:13), they and their fathers to whom Yahweh sent prophets (7:25), continually refused to listen (7:23-36; 9:13; 11:1-4; 13:10; 16:12; 17:23; 19:15). Yahweh issued a curse (11:3) and threats against those who would not heed (17:27). And Yahweh informs Jeremiah that the prophet will not be heard by the people. "You shall call to them and they will not answer you" (7:27). Although this last text approaches rejection, it is little different from that experienced by other prophets, and it is an immeasurable distance from the violent persecution of Jeremiah portrayed so vividly in the confessions.

There is, however, in the call narrative a single, oblique reference to the prophet's fate. "They will fight against you but they will not prevail over you for I am with you" (1:19). Even this text, concerned as it is with the opposition to the prophet, does not prepare the reader for the intense antipathy and violence directed toward Jeremiah in the confessions.

Such sparse attention to the persecution of the prophet in the poetry of cc 1-19 is all the more surprising in view of the strong emphasis given to the theme later in the Book. It is a particularly original feature of this prophetic corpus that the prophet is allowed to voice this strain of the tradition himself until c 20 where the prose narrator introduces it for the first time. (See below.)

In light of this thematic contribution of the confessions, it is noteworthy that the first confession (11:18-12:6) begins with a vivid description of the enemies' attacks upon Jeremiah's life (11:18-20). While the reason for the attacks and the identity of the conspirators are omitted from the confession, information about both is provided by a redactional prose addition, vv 21-23. (See Chapter 1.) The first confession is the only one in which the poetry does not explicitly identify Jeremiah's prophecy as the cause of his persecution. This absence calls forth the editorial comment which tips off the reader to the editor's interest in the confessions. Of equal importance for the commentator of vv 21-23 is the cause of that persecution. The attackers are identified as men of Jeremiah's own village and the motive for their assault is that Jeremiah prophesies in Yahweh's name. This prose addition offers a clue for the interpretation of the confessions in their literary context. The confessions provide concrete evidence that Jeremiah was rejected and persecuted precisely because he was Yahweh's spokesman.

Support for this view comes from the remaining confessions. Each continues the double-edged theme of persecution on account of Jeremiah's prophecy. Jeremiah is cursed (15:10) and persecutors reproach him (15:15 and 17:18). Enemies dig a pit for him (18:20, 22) and plot to slay him (18:22). His persecutors mock him (20:7-8) and conspire to overcome him (20:10). All this treachery is aimed against him because he is a prophet (15:16; 17:15; 18:20b; 20:8-90).[15]

The confessions show, therefore, that the people rejected the prophet, persecuted him and sought consistently to deprive him of his life simply because he was a prophet. If the only extant materials of the Jeremianic traditions were those of cc 1-25, and if the so-called biographical materials of cc 26ff. were lacking, the Book would still testify to the people's refusal to heed the words of the prophet and to their wicked plots to rid the land of him.

B. The Prophet's Requests for Vengeance

A second thematic contribution of the confessions, the prophet's requests for vengeance against his enemies, appears in all five poems.[16] These petitions are calls to Yahweh to fulfill the word spoken through the prophet. (See Chapter 6.) What is at stake is not simply Jeremiah's reputation and dignity, nor even his life, but the validity of his prophetic word, a word that pledges judgment upon a people who have turned away from Yahweh. Jeremiah's concern for vengeance rises to a pitch of intensity in the fourth confession (18:18-23) which is given over almost entirely to the

---

[15]See the preceding chapter for a more thorough discussion of Jeremiah's prophetic role as portrayed in the confessions.

[16]11:20; 12:3; 15:15; 17:18; 18:21, 23; 20:12.

theme. (See Chapter 4.) The final confession (20:7-13) sings in confident triumph that Yahweh will, indeed, effect that vengeance.

The first call for vengeance occurs in the first confession and receives a redactional comment within that confession. (See Chapter 1.) In 11:21-23 Yahweh promises that those who seek to destroy the prophet and simultaneously Yahweh's word, would themselves meet with complete annihilation. Without this redactional comment, one might suppose that the vengeance motif were included in the text only because it was already a part of the confessions. These were installed in the Book for the different purpose of demonstrating that the people rejected the prophet and the vengeance motif was dragged along, too. But the editorial remark (11:21-23) makes such a view unlikely. By calling attention to the theme it apprises the reader upon its first appearance that Jeremiah's requests will be met. The prophet will be vindicated, his enemies destroyed and Yahweh will triumph. The vengeance motif of the confessions obviously engaged the interest of an editor.

The first question raised by the inclusion of Jeremiah's confessions within cc 1-25 is answered in a preliminary manner. The confessions contribute two thematic elements to these chapters, the theme of persecution of the prophet and the theme of petition. It remains to be seen whether these themes contribute to a comprehensive argument of cc 1-25, or if they merely exist in a haphazard fashion among the many other themes in this part of the Book. (See Chapter 8.)

IV. THE RELATIONSHIPS OF THE CONFESSIONS TO THEIR IMMEDIATE LITERARY CONTEXTS

The following survey of the confessions and their placement in the Book indicates that the confessions have been wedded to their immediate literary environs by a variety of procedures. This section describes the literary units within which the confessions are found and then it analyzes the methods used in joining the confessions to their contexts.

The first confession (11:18-12:6) appears within a loosely connected unit (11:1-12:17) composed of the following pieces: a prose sermon cursing those who refuse to listen to the words of the covenant (11:1-14); an oracle of judgment against Israel (11:15-16) with a redactional prose comment (11:17); the confession and its redactional additions (11:18-12:6); twin oracles of judgment against Israel (12:7-9; 10-12); and prose sermon promising hope for the future (12:13-17).

Leaving the confession aside, these assorted materials are themselves unified by a number of literary devices: by the framing motif of listening שמע (11:14; 12:17); by poetic theme of Yahweh's chosen which is imaged by a variety of nouns expressing Israel's uniqueness to Yahweh;[17] by the noun נחלה (12:14) which operates as a motif of the final prose unit (12:14-17) which, in turn, unites the last piece of the passage to the poetry (12:7-9); by the prose comment of 11:17 which identifies the obscure cultic behavior of Israel (11:15) as Baal worship (לקטר לבעל). This comment connects the oracle (11:15-16) to the opening prose sermon (11:1-14) where Israel is also accused of burning incense to Baal (לקטר לבעל v 13; cf., also 12:16).

Even without the confession, 11:1-12:7 exhibits a certain coherence into which the confession is carefully woven by a variety of devices. The confession uses the metaphor of the tree about to be destroyed (11:19 and 12:2) to join the poem to the preceding oracle (11:15-16) in which Israel is imaged as a tree about to be severed by Yahweh's wrath. The confession is also linked to the same oracle (15-16) by the catchword נטע which occurs in 12:2 and in the unifying redactional seam between the two pieces (v 17, see Chapter 1). Furthermore, the confession is connected materially to the poetic oracles which follow it (12:7-9; 10-12) because the two pieces indirectly answer the question "How long will the land mourn?"[18] The confession is further joined to these oracles by the redactional verse 12:6 (see Chapter 1) which employs catchword and motif connections to the confession. In 12:6 Jeremiah's house (ובית-אביך) cries out against him (קראו אחריך מלא). just as Yahweh's house (ביתי 12:7) has raised its voice against Yahweh (נתנה עלי בקולה 12:8). Finally, and of most importance, the confession is joined to its context by the redactional comment of 11:21-23 which relates the confession to a major concern of the prose writer—Israel's refusal to listen to Yahweh's word (11:1-14).

Because he is interested chiefly in Israel's chronic failure to listen, the prose narrator of 11:1-14 plays upon the verb שמע throughout the passage[19] and delivers a curse upon those who refuse (11:3). Meanwhile, the expected blessing for those who do listen is conspicuously absent from the sermon. The writer of this piece is interested only in indicting the people for their deliberate deafness and in listing the concomitant sins which evidence this stubbornness.[20] Although the confession is not linguistically

---

[17]Israel is Yahweh's beloved (ידודי 11:15; ידדות 12:7); his house (ביתי 11:15); his heritage (נחלתי 12:7, 8, 9) and his portion (חלקתי 10a,b).

[18]12:4, אבל, cf., 12:11 and see Chapter 1.

[19]11:2, 3, 4, 6, 7, 8, 10, 14.

[20]Vv 9, 10, 12, 13.

connected to the prose sermon, nor are similar motifs found in the two, the confession functions to illustrate the prose writer's point of view. The people of Israel, indeed the prophet's own kin and townspeople, have rejected the word and persecuted Jeremiah precisely because he was spokesman of the word (11:21-23; 12:6).

Consequently, the first confession is integrated into its context by motif (the tree imagery), by catchwords (נטע, ביתי, אבל), by thematic connections (12:4 and 12:7ff.), by redactional comments 11:21-23 and 12:6), and by its placement which, together with 11:21-23, makes it an illustration of the main concern of the prose sermon (11:1-14)—Israel's failure to hear the word of God.

The second confession (15:10-21) is also carefully inserted into its context though not precisely in the same ways as the first. This confession falls within a loose topical unity,[21] three chapters in length (14-16), which circles about Jeremiah's proclamation that all forms of life in the land are about to cease. C 14 employs a collection of materials on the drought.[22] These develop the theme of the land's inability to support life because of Israel's sins. Cc 15-16 use materials on the women with no future and Jeremiah's confession to develop the theme of the demise of all forms of social life in the land because of Israel's sins.

The second subdivision, wherein the confession appears, comprises the following pieces: a prose sermon describing the futility of prophetic intercession (15:1-4, but see note above); an oracle of judgment relating to the plight of the women (15:5-9); the second confession (15:10-21); and a prose sermon on cessation of social life in the land (16:1-18).

The centerpiece of this collection is the confession, and it is joined to its context in many ways. First, the confession is connected to the other materials in cc 15-16 by the presence of the motif of prophetic intercession which extends across c 15. Prophetic mediation will be powerless to turn Yahweh from his anger (15:1) according to the prose sermon which

---

[21] See Chapter 8 for a discussion of this view of cc 14-15 in relation to Thiel's opinion.

[22] C 14 contains an oracle describing the impact of the drought (vv 2-6); a liturgy seeking the end of the drought (vv 7-9); a refusal of that petition in poetry (v 10) and in prose (vv 11-13); a prose sermon indicting the false prophets (vv 14-16); an oracle of judgment (17-18); a continuation of the liturgy seeking the end of the drought (vv 20-22). The prose of 15:1-4 is probably intended as a further rejection of the people's petition, and if so, also functions to link c 14 to the content and theme of c 15. See below.

bridges cc 14 and 15 (15:1-4). Even if Moses and Samuel were to stand before Yahweh (עמד-י... . . . לפני), the people would still be cast out. Following the prose and its promise of destruction, a poetic oracle (5-9) picks up the intercession motif. Yahweh asks rhetorically who will intercede for Israel now that she has rejected him (15:5). Finally, in Yahweh's reply in the confession, the prophet is promised that if he meets Yahweh's conditions he will be an intercessor, "Before me you will stand" (לפני תעמד, 15:19).

Second, the confession is joined to its context, specifically the preceding oracle of judgment (15:7-9), by sharing catchwords with it: אם (vv 10 and 8) ילד (vv 10 and 9). But the link with the previous poem is more than linguistic; it is also thematic, forming the third link of the confession with its context. The oracle of judgment of vv 7-9 employs imagery focusing on the women of Israel, women who have been widowed or bereaved of children through war, women made barren by larger forces at work within the nation. But this is not human tragedy alone. These women are symbolic of the future of the people for when motherhood ends in tragedy, the life of the nation is also aborted. In this poem that future is abruptly cut off for Yahweh has exterminated his people (v 7). The fate which befalls the women and their cursed offspring, therefore, signals the end of normal, generative life in the land.

The same theme appears in the confession where the prophet's mother is portrayed as similarly fated because she has given birth to a cursed child, a child lacking a future (15:10). But Jeremiah's fate only appears doomed. Unlike the nation, if the prophet meets Yahweh's demands, he will be saved (15:19-21).

Similar thematic links join the confession to c 16. In the confession, Jeremiah's life seems hopeless. He is cursed, a "man of strife and contention" (v 10). He sits alone, outside of social life because of his prophetic call (15:17). The prose writer of c 16 interprets these deprived circumstances of Jeremiah's vocation as symbolic of Israel's fate (16:1-18). Jeremiah's non-participation in social life foreshadows and announces the reality that all social life in the land is at an end. This prose sermon is designed in a midrashic style which both interprets and elaborates v 17 of the confession.[23]

According to the prose writer, Jeremiah was alone because he had been commanded to refrain from marriage and from begetting children (16:3) for an unequivocal reason—family life in the land is cursed (16:13).

---

[23]See Rudolph, *Jeremia*, 110, for a similar assessment of 16:1-9.

Furthermore, Jeremiah was to abstain from participation in social life
(15:17ab), from attending the *marzeach* (16:5), from participating in
mourning rites for the dead (16:6-7) and from celebration and feasts (16:8)
because social life in all its forms would be discontinued in the land (16:9).

In connection with this grim comparison of the fate of the nation with
the vocational hardships of the prophet, the people are indicted for the sin
of idolatry committed by their ancestors. But their far greater crime and
the cause of these bleak prognostications for the future was Israel's
refusal to listen (16:12). Once again, therefore, the juxtaposition of the
prose sermon with the confession indicates that the confessions serve to
provide testimony by the suffering and rejected prophet that Israel willfully, chronically, and stubbornly rejected the prophet and his message.

Consequently, the second confession, like the first, is embedded in its
context by catchwords (אם and ילד) and by shared motifs (prophetic intercession and bereaved women). But of more importance, the prose writer
uses themes of the confession to develop the picture of Israel's future: life
in the land was doomed. Moreover, the prose writer's accusation that the
people refused to listen seems closely associated with the confession's
depiction of the rejection of the prophet.

The third confession (17:14-18) is far more difficult to establish in its
immediate context than the first two. C 17 comprises a short prose sermon promising holocaust and exile (17:1-4);[24] a poem on the themes of
cursing and blessing in relation to trust (17:5-8); a poetic assertion that
Yahweh is the Judge of hearts (17:9-10);[25] a wisdom saying about the rich
fool (17:11); a liturgical fragment (17:12-13); the third confession (17:14-
18); a prose sermon on keeping the Sabbath (17:19-27).

Despite their best efforts, scholars cannot find a unifying element in
this chapter. However, some of the poetry is linked together by the catchword לב (17:1b; 5b; 9a; 10a), and the liturgical fragment (12-13) may be
connected to the previous wisdom saying (v 11) by the catchword עזב (11c;
12b,d), but neither catchword occurs in the confession. The word בוש is
employed in 13b and twice in 18, but this is the only evidence of similar
vocabulary between the confession and its context. Unlike the first two
confessions, common images or motifs do not link this one to the

---

[24]See the critical discussion of this passage and its doublet under text-
critical notes.

[25]It is possible that these verses form the concluding stanza of the previous poem.

surrounding materials. What the context of the third confession shares with the other two confessions is the presence of a prose sermon (19-27) which emphasizes the theme of listening while it enjoins Israel to keep the Sabbath. Furthermore, the word שמע appears frequently in this sermon (17:20, 23, 24, 27) as it did in the previously examined sermons located near a confession.

While a confession is juxtaposed once again with a prose passage concerned with Israel's failure to listen, the third confession is not intrinsically connected with its context. It is not at all likely, then, that the third confession was joined to its context during the oral stage of the transmission process since the text exhibits none of the typical connecting devices of that process. Rather the third confession's only firm connection with its context seems to be that of the broad topical relationship with the prose sermon imploring Israel to listen to Yahweh's word, a link created by the juxtaposition of the texts.

The fourth (18:18-23) and the fifth (20:7-13) confessions are located within the most tightly shaped unit of the entire section of cc 11-20. The unit, comprising all of cc 18-20 and joined together by a narrative thread (see Chapter 8) is composed of the following literary materials: a prose sermon on the occasion of Jeremiah's visit to the potter's house (18:1-12); a poetic oracle of judgment (18:13-17); the fourth confession (18:18-23); a prose sermon on the occasion of the breaking of the flask (19:1-15); the prose sermon on the occasion of Jeremiah's imprisonment in the stocks (20:1-6); the fifth and final confession (20:7-13); a cursing poem (20:14-18).

The fourth confession is connected to the immediately surrounding material in two ways. The redactional comment of 18:18 (see Chapter 4) secures the confession in its context. It joins it to the opening prose sermon (18:1-12) through the use of the catchword חשב which appears twice in 18a and twice in the prose sermon (18:11, 12). This prose comment (18:18) is itself skillfully linked to the confession by the same catchword, חשב, which appears in the last clause of 18 and in the first word of 19. An important feature of v 18 is that, like 11:21-23, it functions as a midrash upon the confession to provide the now familiar motive for the enemies' persecution of Jeremiah—the elimination of his prophecy from earshot.

Delivered upon the occasion of Jeremiah's visit to the Potter's House, the prose sermon of 18:1-13 announces a threat from Yahweh (vv 6, 7, 10-11), the enactment of which is contingent upon failure of the people to repent. Evidence of such a failure would be their refusal to listen (שמע) to Yahweh (v 10). To Jeremiah's final appeal for amendment, the nation answers with a decisive "no" (v 12). The confession is joined to these last two verses (11-12) by the catchwords in v 12. This confession, therefore, like the previous three confessions, substantiates the prose writer's contention that despite Yahweh's warning to the people, they refused to hear (v 18) and conspired to entrap his prophet (18:20, 22).

The fourth confession is juxtaposed with another prose narrative: the account of the symbolic action[26] of the breaking of the flask and its interpretive sermon (c 19). The connection of the confession to this prose material is not basically linguistic; only עצה in the confession (18:23, 18) is repeated (19:7), nor is the linkage forged by repeated motifs or images. Again, the connection is thematic. In the confession the prophet requests vengeance upon his enemies. In the prose Yahweh commands the breaking of the flask heralding Israel's destruction because the people refused to listen (שמע) to his word (19:15). The prophet's petition for vindication and vengeance in the confession is immediately answered by the prose (see Chapter 8). Again the prose narrative is concerned with Israel's refusal to listen.

This brief survey of the location of the fourth confession in its context reveals that it exhibits only minimal catchword connection with the surrounding material. These connections are not created by the poetry of the confession but by the redactional prose addition to the confession (18:18). Like the first three confessions, the fourth one is closely related to prose materials which denounce Israel for what has become a cliched offense: her willful deafness to Yahweh's word.

The fifth and last confession (20:7-13) is associated with the immediately preceding prose narrative (20:1-6) by the catchword מגור מסביב (10b, 3), but this is the only technical link between the two pieces. Of the five confessions, this one alone is provided with a precise narrative setting by a prose account. This particular prose account is very important because in it, for the first time in the Book, evidence is provided for the persecution and rejection of the prophet in material other than the confessions. In the narrative, the catchword from the confession (מגור מסביב) forms a play on words to condemn the priest Pashur and his associates. Pashur prophesied falsely, leading his friends astray, and they in turn are guilty because they listened (שמע) to him (20:6). In this narrative, therefore, the prose writer has given his own account of Israel's refusal to listen to Yahweh's word. The nation rejected and persecuted Yahweh's

---

[26]See Chapter 8 for a discussion of symbolic actions.

representative, and chose to listen, instead, to the words of the "false prophet."

Immediately following this account, the confession offers further evidence of Jeremiah's persecution (7c,d, 10), it repeats his request for vengeance (v 12), and, for the first time, it expresses his confidence that Yahweh's word will triumph (vv 11-13). The latter element of the confession will be a critical component of the structure of cc 1-25.

The fifth confession, therefore, exhibits only one catchword connection to the preceding prose narrative but, because that phrase is at once enigmatic and ironic when applied to Pashur, 20:1-6 can be understood as a midrash developed around this catchword, just as 16:1-13 seems best explained as a midrashic elaboration upon 15:17. Although such a connection of the relationship of the two pieces is uncertain, it is not uncertain that the confession once again provides evidence of the persecution and rejection of the prophet and his word.

This brief analysis of the confessions' relationship to their immediate literary contexts can be summarized as follows:

1. No single procedure has been employed to join the confessions to the prose and poetry surrounding them, but rather a variety of connecting devices weld the confessions to the larger corpus.

a.) Three confessions are joined to their contexts by means of catchwords (11:18-12:6; 15:10-21; 20:7-13). In the placement of the third and fourth confessions (17:14-18; 18:18-23), this connecting device seems to little or no importance. The catchword bridge between the fifth confession and the prose narrative of 20:1-6 may be explained as a prose expansion or midrash upon מגור מסביב of the confession, rather than a device connecting two separate pieces of oral tradition. Even more certainly, 16:1-13 appears to be a midrashic comment upon 15:17 and so joins it to its context.

b.) The first two confessions (11:18-12:6 and 15:10-21) share images and motifs with their surrounding contexts. The first confession utilizes the image of the tree found also in 11:15-16; the second confession uses the mother with cursed offspring motif in common with the preceding poem (15:5-9) and the motif of prophetic intercession found also in 15:1-4.

c.) The first (11:18-12:6) and fourth (18:18-23) confessions are woven into their contexts by means of redactional comments added to the confessions (11:21-23; 12:6; 18:18). All these additions are midrashic in style; that is, they make specific those situations which are left vague and imprecise in the body of the poems. All speak of the persecution of Jeremiah, and two identify his prophesy as the reason for the persecution (11:21-23; 18:18).

2. There is one characteristic of the contexts of all the confessions, however, which requires special attention. By virtue of their locations, all five appear closely connected with prose sermons which, in turn, are concerned with Israel's refusal to listen to the word of Yahweh: 11:18-12:6 follows closely upon 11:1-14, the curse upon those who refuse to listen; 15:1-21 is succeeded by 16:1-13, the description of the end of social life in the land because Israel has not listened; 17:14-18 precedes 17:19-27, the injunction to keep the Sabbath and to listen; 18:18-23 follows 18:1-12, the appeal at the potter's house for Israel to repent and to listen; this same confession is followed by 19:1-15, the breaking of the flask when elders and priests refused to listen; 20:7-13 succeeds 20:1-6, the imprisonment of the prophet and the accusation against the false prophet to whom the people sinfully listened. Each of these prose sections employs the verb שמע, some quite frequently,[27] and all indict Israel for what appears to be, in the perspective of the prose writer, Israel's overriding crime: its willful deafness to Yahweh's word.

This summary of the relationships of the confessions to their immediate literary contexts leads to the following conclusions:

1. The lack of uniformity in the means employed to merge the confessions with their contexts presents a problem to the interpreter of the confessions. On the one hand, such unevenness in the use of connecting devices suggests that the five poems were inserted into the Jeremianic traditions during the oral stages of transmission and without the operation of conscious literary principles. On the other hand, the complete absence of catchword connections, or motif and thematic links between the third and fourth confessions and their

---

[27]Cf., 11:1-14, for example.

contexts creates an anomaly for such a theory since none of the usual principles of oral bonding of materials appear operative in either case.

2. The regularity with which the confessions are placed near or next to prose narratives which decry Israel's failure to heed God's word, combined with the observation that the confessions contribute evidence of Israel's rejection of the prophet and his message, argues for a deliberate literary incorporation of the confessions into the Book. The possible midrashic relationship of 16:1-13 and 20:1-6 to their neighboring confessions, and the explicit connection drawn to the theme of the prophet's persecution by the redactional prose comments of 11:21-23 and 18:18 adds strength to this view. The midrashic style of the redactional additions to the confessions (11:21-23; 12:6; 18:18) confirms the recognition that 16:1ff. and 20:1ff. are midrashic and that all come from the same hand.

In light of these observations it can be concluded that the confessions were incorporated into the Jeremianic traditions at the redactional stage by the prose writer to illustrate his indictment of Israel and to explain the disaster which finally overtook the nation.

Such an assessment of the confessions' purpose within their literary contexts expands their original purpose of the authentication of the prophet. They now provide evidence of the people's crimes, an implicit indictment which forms part of a larger argument to explain the Fall of the nation.

This explanation of the confessions' incorporation into the text leaves some important questions unanswered. Why were the confessions separated from one another since the same thematic contribution might have been made by including the poems as a unified collection? Why were the separated pieces placed only within the cc 11-20 rather than distributed more broadly within the Book or incorporated with the prose traditions concerning the persecution of the prophet, the so-called B materials in cc 26ff.?

Any attempt to answer these questions requires an analysis of the arrangement of the materials in cc 1-25. This will reveal a structural reason for the peculiar placement of the poems. Before proceeding to such an analysis, scholarly opinion regarding the arrangment of the materials in cc 1-25 must be reviewed.

8

The Role of the Confessions
in Chapters 1–25

I. THE REASONS FOR THE PLACEMENT
OF THE CONFESSIONS IN CC 11-20

Scholarly perspectives on the arrangement of the materials in the Book of Jeremiah reach little more agreement than theories regarding the composition of the Book. Cornill, for instance, is not alone in holding the opinion that no Old Testament Book is as devoid of structure as the Book of Jeremiah.[1] Even Bright warns the readers of his commentary that Jeremiah exhibits no plan beyond "grand and obvious divisions into books"[2] and these, collected topically, reveal little evidence of inner arrangement.[3] He labels cc 1-25 as simply "words of censure, warning and judgment."[4]

In a similar vein, Rudolph understood the Book's arrangement according to large divisions[5] and, like Bright, argues that cc 1-25 contain a collection of various materials thematically connected.[6] But for Rudolph, the Book also reveals a literary pattern in its broadest arrangement because it is fashioned after Isaiah 1-35 and the Book of Ezekiel.

As with the theories of composition of the Book, these descriptions of

---

[1] Cornill, *Das Buch*, XXXVII; see also Condamin's view including his discussion of the similar opinion of Jerome and Theodoret in *Le Livre*, XVI-XVII.

[2] 1-25:13; 46-51; 30-37; 26-29; 34-45, 52.

[3] Bright, AB, XVII-LIX.

[4] Ibid., LIX.

[5] 1-25:14; 25:15-38; 46-51; 36-45.

[6] Rudolph, *Jeremia*, XIX-XX, also agrees with the earlier view that cc 1-25 are arranged in general chronological order: cc 1-6, Josiah; 7-20, Jehoiakim; 21-24, later period; 25:1-14, fourth year of Jehoiakim.

its structure are derived largely from a form-critical approach to the text. Heavy emphasis is placed upon accidental connections, and traditions are understood to be organized to assist memories of oral tradents rather than for literary purposes.

Unfortunately, most recent studies are not concerned with the structure of the Book. They focus on the genesis of the text, the alleged contents of the *Urrolle*[7] or analysis and identification of sources used by redactors.[8] Thiel's[9] and Pohlmann's[10] works are the exceptions. Though they do address the question of sources, they also analyze large portions of the Book with a view to recovering possible literary structures. Pohlman's work concentrates on the prose materials after c 20 and so has little direct bearing on the argument of this chapter. However, Thiel's redaction-critical study represents a major advance over the earlier studies regarding the arrangement of the materials in cc 1-25.

Readily acknowledging catchword and thematic connections of the material, Thiel moves beyond them to find evidence of literary purpose in the arrangement of materials in cc 11-20. He observes that the first and last units (11:1-12:6 and cc 18-20) and, more tentatively, the central unit (cc 14-15) exhibit a similar formal pattern in the ordering of their content. This conscious design presents stylized scenes of Jeremiah's typical preaching. Thiel's schema follows:[11]

Occasion for Preaching	11:1-6	14:1-9 19-22	18:1-4	19:1ff.
Message of Judgment	11:7-17	14:10-18 15:1-9	18:5-17	19:3-15

---

[7]Holladay, *Architecture*; Claus Rietzschel, *Das Problem der Urrolle: Ein Beitrag zur Redaktionsgeschichte des Jeremiabuches* (Gütersloh: Gütersloher Verlagshaus Gerd Mohn, 1966).

[8]Gunther Wanke, *Untersuchungen zur sogenannten Baruchschrift*, BZAW 122 (Berlin: Walter de Gruyter, 1971); Helga Weippert, *Die Prosareden des Jeremiabuches*, BZAW 132 (Berlin: Walter de Gruyter, 1973); Nicholson, *Preaching*.

[9]Thiel, *Die Deuteronomistische Redaktion*, I.

[10]Karl-Friedrich Pohlman, *Studien zum Jeremiabuch: Ein Beitrag zur Frage nach der Entstehung des Jeremiahbuches*, FRLANT 118 (Göttingen: Vandenhoeck & Ruprecht, 1978).

[11]Thiel, *Die Deuteronomistische Redaktion*, I, 287.

(Word of Judgment)	11:15ff.	14:17ff. 15:5-9	18:13-17	19:10,11a
Persecution of prophet	11:18-23	15:10, 15	18:18	20:1-6
Lament	12:6	15:10f.	18:19-23	20:7-18

Though his investigation represents a methodological advance, Thiel's categories are unsatisfactory because they are vague and applied without respect for the literary forms present in the passages. A few examples will illustrate the problems. When applied to 11:1-6, for instance, "the occasion for preaching" (*Anlass zur Verkündigung*) is incorrect because all but v 1 records the preaching itself. The category "persecution of the prophet" (*Verfolgung*) is correctly applied to 18:18 and 20:1-6, but persecution is also found in 18:20, 22 and in 20:7-10 which are not included in the category. The laments (*Klage*) are likewise misidentified by the omission of 11:18-23 and by the inclusion of 20:14-18 (see Chapters 1 and 5). In addition, the word of judgment (*Gerichtswort*), a subdivision of the message of judgment (*Gerichtsbotschaft*), which label 18:13-17 and 11:15-17, refers to poetic oracles only, while the same label for 19:10-11a applies to prose narrative material.

Thiel's proposal fails particularly in his treatment of cc 14 and 15 because his schema cannot account adequately for the liturgical piece of 14:19-22, which he identifies as an occasion for preaching.[12] Nor can his schema provide a suitable description of the shift in 14:11 from poetic oracle of judgment to narrative dialogue,[13] a shift which also changes the subject from accusation and punishment (v 10) to a discussion of the false prophets. A final objection to Thiel's argument is that his schematic description of the arrangement of cc 11-20 overlooks the narrative unity of cc 18-20 (see below), and fails to see the broad topical unity created by cc 14-16. (See Chapter 7.) Consequently, while his redaction-critical method is helpful in raising new questions about the literary shape of cc 11-20, Thiel's schematic description of these chapters does not fit the literature, nor does his work give adequate attention to the role of the confessions in the argument and structure of cc 11-20.

---

[12]Ibid., 287-289.
[13]Ibid.

Nor is Westermann's proposal any more satisfactory.[14] He argues that the confessions are redactionally placed to represent Jeremiah's response to the commissioning passage in cc 11-20. This thesis fails to explain the placement of the confessions. It is true that Yahweh gives precise commands to Jeremiah in these passages (11:1-14; 14:1-15:4; 16:1-13; 18:1-12; 19:1-20:6). However, these passages contain sermonic and symbolic materials which have little to do with the commissions in question. C 14, for instance, pays more attention to the liturgy and the drought than to Jeremiah's negative commission not to pray for the people; 20:1-6 contains no commission, only symbolic activity and sermon. The *Auftrage* category, therefore, is an inadequate designation for these texts. Moreover, c 13, which recounts the commission to bury the loincloth cannot be accounted for in Westermann's theory because it contains no confession. Another solution is necessary. It is the thesis of this chapter that the confessions provide a key to the structural arrangement of the Jeremiah traditions in this section of the Book, and that this arrangement does more than simply stylize the preaching of the prophet or describe the prophet's response to Yahweh's commissions. It presents an argument regarding the destruction of the nation and the justice of God.

Before turning to the structural role of the confessions in cc 11-20, it is first necessary to give attention to the components of the broader literary unit of cc 1-25.[15] Cc 1-25 comprise the following parts, each of which will be treated below:

A. c 1	Introduction: The Call Narrative
B. cc 2-10	Jeremiah's Appeals to the Nation
C. cc 11-20	Jeremiah's Final Appeals and Rejection
D. cc 21-24	Appendices Concerning the Situation
	After the Fall of the Nation
E. 25:1-13	Summary[16]

A. The Call Narrative

The call narrative of c 1 is a redactional composition, long recognized

---

[14]Claus Westermann, *Jeremia* (Stuttgart: Calwer, 1967).

[15]That cc 1-25 form a unit or "book" within the larger corpus has been broadly acknowledged. See Bright, AB, LVII; Rudolph, *Jeremia*, XIX; Thiel, *Die deuteronomistische Redaktion*, I.

[16]Cf., note 14.

as a collection of originally disparate pieces,[17] which sounds all the major themes to appear in cc 1-25. The chapter can be divided as follows: vv 1-3, the superscription to the entire Jeremianic corpus; vv 4-10, the call account proper; vv 11-16, report of two inaugural visions; vv 17-19, final commission and assurance. Since it is generally agreed that the call account in vv 4-10 is distinct from the visions,[18] the call and its relationship to the confessions must be addressed first. Then the purpose of the rest of the chapter in relation to cc 1-25 can be considered.

The call account proper (vv 4-10) presents many problems to the exegete. For one thing, it combines prose and poetry in strange ways to suggest an editor's involvement. As many scholars have observed,[19] only the words of Yahweh are rhythmical (vv 5, 7, 8, 9c and possibly 10), while the prophet's responses to Yahweh are expressed in prose (vv 6, 7a, 9ab). Moreover, in v 10, the meter of Yahweh's speech is disturbed by the apparent addition of ולהאביד ולהרוס[20] which intrudes upon the chiasm created by the rest of the series of infinitive constructs.[21] Furthermore, v 10 repeats and expands the idea נביא לגוים נתתיך of v 5. There is also the problem of the dependence of 7d ואת כל-אשר אצוך תדבר and 9d נתתי דברי בפיו ודבר אליהם את כל-אשר אצונו upon Dt 18:18 דברי בפיך. Finally, it has been solidly established[22] that vv 4-10 follow, with some variation, the conventional call narrative *Gattung*. Much of this evidence —the conventional formal arrangement of the material, the dependence on Dt 18:18, the peculiar arrangement of prose and poetry, the expansion

---

[17]Cf., Bright, AB, 6-8; Duhm, *Das Buch*, 1-2; Reventlow, *Liturgie*, 77; Rudolph, *Jeremia*, 21-31; Thiel, *Die Deuteronomistische Redaktion*, I, 63-79; Nicholson, CBC, 23-24.

[18]See, for example, Nicholson, CBC, 21; Weiser, *Das Buch*, 14; J. A. Thompson, *The Book of Jeremiah* (Grand Rapids: William B. Eerdmans, 1980).

[19]For example, Thiel, *Die Deuteronomistische Redaktion*, I, 63; Carroll, *From Chaos*, 44.

[20]See text-critical note in BHS.

[21]See Thiel, *Die deuteronomistische Redaktion*, I, 69; Nicholson, CBC, 24; William L. Holladay, *Jeremiah: Spokesman Out of Time*, Pilgrim Press Book (Philadelphia: United Church Press, 1974) 28-29. The infinitive constructs of v 10 occur frequently throughout the Book but only in prose (2:14-17; 17:7-10; 24:5-7; 31:27-28; 32:10; 45:4). See also Nicholson, *Preaching*, 115.

[22]Norman C. Habel, "The Form and Significance of the Call Narratives," *ZAW* 77 (1965) 297-323 and Carroll, *From Chaos*, 31-58.

created by v 10—points to the possibility that the whole piece is the work of an editor.

On the other hand, the presence of large pieces of poetry makes it difficult to exclude the prophet's own words and experience from the core of the passage. Additions have expanded it. For a number of reasons v 10 is one of these: it functions to describe the whole prophetic corpus; its meter is disturbed; it appears again only in the prose and, it functions as an expansion of v 5. The citation of Dt 18:18 in 7d and 9d may also signal the adjustments of an editor.[23] Though the nature of the evidence makes it impossible to be too dogmatic about the text's genesis, one can conclude with caution that the words of prophet and redactor are artfully intermingled in this important passage.

Despite the difficulty of establishing authorship vv 4-10 exhibit some curious resemblances to the confessions. Though linguistic connections are minimal and inconclusive, two inguistic features common to both may be significant. The verb "to know" (ידע) appears in vv 5 and 6, and in v 5, at least, carries the same connotations of intimate covenant relationship as it does in the confessions.[24] In vv 6, 7, 8 emphatic personal pronouns are used by Yahweh and the prophet, a stylistic feature commonly employed in the confessions.[25] The simple fact of common subject matter may explain other linguistic links between the call and the confessions.[26]

It is the link between the call and the confessions created by this common subject matter which is of most importance. As in the confessions, the focus of the call narrative is Jeremiah's prophetic vocation. In both Jeremiah's resistance is emphatically underscored. In the call he is a נער who does not know how to conduct the prophet's chief activity, speaking (v 6). Yahweh knows (ידעתיך) him before his birth (v 5). He is made a prophet solely at Yahweh's initiative. Yahweh called him at conception (v 5), and therefore, Jeremiah had nothing at all to do with the assumption of his role; he was compelled to accept a prenatal assignment (v 7). And he is assured that success in his role will be the result of Yahweh's presence (v 8). Vv 9 and 10 reemphasize elements of vv 4-8. V. 9 reiterates

---

[23]But see Holladay, "Jeremiah and Moses: Further Observations," *JBL* 85 (March 1966) 17-27, who places this identification with Moses in Jeremiah's consciousness.

[24]11:18, two times; 11:19; 12:3; 15:15; 17:16; 18:23. Cf., Chapter 6.

[25]11:19, 20; 12:5; 15:19; 17:14, 15, 16, 17, 18; 18:20, 23.

[26]קדש in 1:5 and 12:3; הנה in 1:5, 9 and 17:15; the verb דבר in 1:6, 7, 9 and 12:1, 20:8, 9 and the noun in 15:16, 17:15 and 20:8; יד in 1:9 and 15:17; and כי in 1:9, 12:2 and 15:19.

the circumstance that Jeremiah's word is not his own but Yahweh's, and v 10 repeats and expands v 5.[27]

By its citation of Dt 18:18, the call account also presents Jeremiah as the prophet like Moses. This similarity of Jeremiah's call account to Moses' induction to divine service has not gone unnoticed by scholars.[28] Moses also resisted, expressed impotence with regard to speech and was forced to accept his calling (Ex 3)—themes already discovered in the confessions. Despite Holladay's insistence to the contrary, one cannot easily decide whether this pattern of Mosaic compulsion/resistance in Jeremiah's call existed in Jeremiah's consciousness or was the interpretation of a redactor. However, if 7d and 9d are editorial expansions, it was an editor who wished to make this connection explicit by adding 7d and 9d.[29] What is clear is that the confessions stand within the same prophetic tradition, employing the same motifs to a similar end.

The call narrative account proper (vv 4-10), therefore, functions to legitimate the prophet in the same way that the confessions establish his authenticity as Yahweh's spokesman. Yet the call narrative differs formally from the confessions. Each of them employs part or all of the psalm of individual lament form, while this passage utilizes the conventional call narrative form.[30]

As a consequence, the relationship of the account of the call to the confessions must be found in content and not in form. If at least the nucleus of the call narrative proper originated with the prophet as the presence of poetry argues, then the call account served a function similar to the confessions within the life of the prophet. It identified the prophet as a true spokesman of Yahweh who was drafted unwillingly and who received all impetus and content for his mission from Yahweh.

Yet it differs somewhat from the confession in not referring to the persecution of the prophet, except perhaps in a proleptic manner in v 8 where the prophet is exhorted not to fear a mysterious "them." Unlike the confession, the hypothetical original function of the call narrative remains its function in its present location in the Book. The call account proper, along with the rest of c 1 (see below), continue to serve as

---

[27]See Thiel, *Die Deuteronomistische Redaktion,* I, 69.

[28]See Habel, "The Form" and Carroll, *From Chaos,* 33-34, and especially Holladay, "The Background of Jeremiah's Self-Understanding: Moses, Samuel and Psalm 22," *JBL* 83 (1964) 153-164 and "Jeremiah and Moses, Further Considerations," *JBL* 85 (1966) 17-27.

[29]See Thiel, *Die Deuteronomistische Redaktion,* I, 63.

[30]Cf., Habel, "The Form."

authenticating credentials for all that is to follow in the Book. In this chapter, Jeremiah is identified as a reliable and vindicated messenger of the divine.[31]

After establishing the credentials of the prophet, the call narrative relates two of Jeremiah's inaugural visions. Both introduce major themes of the subsequent chapters and add authority to his prophetic claims. In the first vision of the almond tree, Yahweh interprets the puzzle of the word play (שָׁקֵד, v 11; שֹׁקֵד v 12). He "is watching over his word to accomplish it" (v 12). This is a major theme of cc 2-25 which present an account of the delivery of accomplishment of that word in the life of the nation. (See below.) The second inaugural vision of the boiling pot is related to the first vision. It describes how Yahweh will fulfill that word. Yahweh will call forth the families of the Kingdoms of the North who will establish hegemony over Judah, and Yahweh will use them as judges to indict the people. The people's offense—blatant idolatry.

In vv 17-19 the visions are left behind and attention turns from the content of the message back to the role of the prophet. He is commanded to speak the entire message to the people and not "to break" (חתת) before them (v 17). In words of assurance (18-19), Yahweh promises him that he will be strengthened before the people who will fight against him (v 18), but Yahweh will not give the enemies the victory (v 19). The call narrative, therefore, closes on the theme of the people's rejection of the prophet. This theme develops the assurance of v 8 by promising the prophet's triumph despite rejection. At the same time, it implicitly indicts the people for refusing to accept one with the unmistakable authority of a true prophet of Yahweh.

This opening programmatic chapter announces all the major themes of cc 1-25.[32] The prophet is authenticated as Yahweh's true herald. Yahweh promises to accomplish the word given to the prophet. That word will involve invasion by a mysterious people from the North who will be an instrument of Yahweh's judgment, a judgment brought on by the nation's idolatry and disobedience.

Subsequent discussion will illustrate how these themes develop in the

---

[31]Such a claim might have been a prerequisite for the acceptance of the Book among the Exilic community for whom the discernment of the true prophet was more than a pressing concern. Cf., Ezek 12 and 13; Nicholson, *Preaching*, 126; and Frank Lothar Hossfeld and Ivo Meyer, *Prophet Gegen Prophet*, 141-142.

[32]See Nicholson, *Preaching*, 115, for a similar view of the chapter as late and anticipatory.

overall unit of cc 2-25 and special attention is given to the contributions of the confessions to that development. Cc 2-10 are analyzed according to form, content and structure to determine why they lack confessions. Next, cc 11-20 are examined according to form, content and structure to discover why they include confessions. Finally, cc 21-25 are surveyed to determine how these chapters relate to cc 11-20 and thereby confirm or disconfirm the thesis of this chapter.

B. Cc 2-10: Jeremiah's Appeal to the Nation

Three characteristics of cc 2-10 serve to distinguish it from cc 11-20, form-critical and thematic components and structural arrangement.

1. Form-Critical Components

Form-critically, cc 2-10 are composed predominantly of poetry with relatively few prose interruptions.[33] Of these prose passages, only one, the Temple Sermon (7:1-8:3), is a long prose account similar to those found in abundance in cc 11-20. This means that little interpretive comment on the prophet's message appears in this section of the Book. Instead, the poetry of the prophet is left to speak for itself.

2. Thematic Components

With respect to content, cc 2-10 contain many appeals to people to repent, to amend their ways before it is too late,[34] so many, in fact, that these provide a key for interpreting the unit.

In cc 2-4 Jeremiah's call to the people to turn away from their sins is cast in generally conciliatory terms. The prophet appeals to Yahweh's former gracious treatment of them (2:3, 6-7a, 11b, 31; 3:19) and to the former devotion of Israel (2:1-3), begging the nation to return to Yahweh (3:12-14, 19-23; 4:1-4, 13-14). In cc 2-4, therefore, threats of judgment and promises of disaster appear designed as warnings, indications of what might happen if Israel fails to repent, rather than as announcements of certain doom.[35]

---

[33]3:6-11, 15-18, 24-25; 4:9-12; 7:1-8:3; 9:12-16, 23-25.

[34]Cf., c 2; 3:12, 14, 22; 4:1-4, 12-14; 5:1-17; 6:8; 7:3-15.

[35]Cf., Thomas M. Raitt, *A Theology of Exile: Judgment/Deliverance in Jeremiah and Ezekiel* (Philadelphia: Fortress, 1977) 39, who argues for a

C 5 confirms such motivation behind the initial presentation of Jeremiah's prophecy but it also increases the somberness of the preaching. The prophet is commanded to search the streets of Jerusalem to find a faithful follower of Yahweh (5:1-3) and to visit every strata of society in his search (vv 4-5). There are no faithful to be found. Apostasy has infected the entire society, so punishment appears unavoidable (5:6). Yet Yahweh mournfully resists punishing the people (v 7). In the refrain repeated across several chapters, "Shall I not punish them for these things? Shall I not avenge myself on a nation such as this?" (5:9, 29: 9:9), and which accompanies catalogues of Israel's sins,[36] Yahweh seems to be convincing himself against his own desires and instincts that punishment is his only recourse.[37]

In subsequent chapters, Yahweh continues to pursue the people through the prophet,[38] and the people continue to reject him.[39] Threats of war, destruction related to harvests and disasters which accompany invasion[40] are interspersed with these appeals and accusations. The threats and promises of disaster notwithstanding, the abundance of invitations to repent indicate that the oracles of doom are best understood as conditional warnings which hinge on the nation's reform. A consideration of cc 11-20 where appeals diminish and then disappear will confirm this interpretation. (See below.)

After the refrain (9:9, 5:9, 29), however, there are no more expressions of reluctance to punish and no more explicit calls to repent within this unit of the Book. Instead, the mourning women are summoned to sing dirges for a people about to become a corpse at a funeral (9:10-22). C 10 ends this first unit of the Book with enigmatic liturgical pieces.[41] These

---

first stage in Jeremiah's preaching in which there was still time to accept salvation. Accordingly, these appeals ("summons to repentance"), represent a basic speech pattern. Raitt makes no distinction, however, between prose and poetry in his identification of this form.

[36] 5:7-8, 21-28, 30-31; 8:4-15; 9:4-8 and cf., 6:13-15.

[37] See Raitt, A Theology, 25-28, for a discussion of the tension between Yahweh's judgment and mercy expressed in this formula, and see p. 97 for a similar interpretation of the refrain under discussion here.

[38] 5:22, 6:8, 10a, 16abc, 17a; 8:6a, 13.

[39] 5:23-24; 6:10bc, 16d, 17b; 8:6b, 13bc.

[40] 4:5-8, 23-31; 5:6, 10, 14-17; 6:1-6, 9, 11, 19-21, 22-26; 8:9-10, 12cd, 16-17; 9:7-9. See note 40.

[41] The liturgical pieces (10:6-10), 12-16, 23-25) can be understood as the expression of the false worship of a faithless Israel who mouths orthodoxy

poems surround an oracle promising the imminent arrival of the foe from the North.

This brief description reveals that the poetry of cc 2-10 changes tone from conciliation and warning to judgment and impending punishment. Yet in cc 2-10 even threats of judgment are left mysteriously unspecified.[42] This progression toward doom in the prophecy suggests that this material is, indeed, arranged in broad chronological order, growing more ominous as appeals for conversion fail. In addition, the relative dearth of prose interruptions in comparison to those in cc 11-20 (see below), argues that the prophet's message is permitted to speak for itself with little attempt to interpret it, adapt it or to report how it was received by its audience.

A comparison of the one major prose passage of this unit, the Temple Sermon and its embellishments (7:1-8:3), with the c 26 account of the same event confirms this view. Of particular note in c 7 is the complete absence of any report of the human response to the Sermon, a response which is the major concern of the c 26 account. There the description of the Sermon's content is limited to two verses (26:4-6). In c 7 the content of the Sermon is greatly extended and the response is completely eliminated. The two accounts serve different purposes. The c 26 version is

---

but lives sinfully. To its pleas for Yahweh's favors, Yahweh replies no, a no expressed by the juxtaposition of the liturgy with prophecies of doom (10:17, 18, 19-21, 22). On the other hand, this liturgy would make more sense understood as an Exilic insertion because it praises Yahweh as the one true God over all the nations (vv 6-7, 10), in control of nature (10, 12-13), and whose power reveals the falseness of all idols (8, 9, 14, 15, 16a). And Yahweh is asked to modulate the punishment (v 24), not to destroy Israel totally and to turn anger against the nations which have destroyed Israel (v 25). See Rudolph, *Jeremia,* 71, for a discussion of scholarly views, most of which deny this passage to Jeremiah, and most of which, including Rudolph's, place the liturgy in the Exile or after.

Similarly, the prose insertions promising hope and salvation (3:6-18; 5:18-19) would seem most at home after the Fall of Jerusalem. It is true that 3:6-18, which includes a poetic piece, may well incorporate appeals by Jeremiah to the people of the North to return during the time of Josiah. See Holladay, *Jeremiah,* 47. But these verses could also be interpreted as indictment of Judah for failing to learn the lesson of the Fall of Samaria and conclude with hope for a restored and united nation after the Exile. But the text provides inadequate evidence for a firm decision on the matter.

[42]For example, "a great commotion from the land of the North" in 10:22 (cf., 6:22-26); "death and destruction" in 9:17-22 (cf., 8:10).

a conflict story designed to lead off the following series of prose narratives where the prophet frequently collides with the authorities and with the community (cf., cc 27-29).

The subject matter of the c 7 version is Israel's cultic misbehavior in relation to the Temple (vv 1-15), to the cult of the queen of heaven (vv 16-20), to burnt offerings (vv 21-26) and to the doings at Topheth (vv 30-34). However, interspersed with these specific cultic condemnations are themes common to the prose of cc 11-20. Israel, for instance, is warned not to go after or is accused of going after other gods.[43] The nation is indicted for burning incense to Baal[44] or offering sacrifices to Baal.[45] Reference is made to the sins of the fathers[46] and the people are reminded that Yahweh brought them from Egypt.[47] They are accused of refusing to listen[48] and of following their own stubborn hearts[49] even though Yahweh persistently sent them prophets.[50] Because of their sins, the prophet is commanded not to pray for this people.[51] All joy in the land will come to an end[52] and punishment will come in the form of unquenchable fire.[53] The punished will be as dung on the surface of the ground.[54] No one will bury them[55] and Topheth will be the scene of an unspeakable curse.[56]

A major purpose of the Temple Sermon of c 7 is, therefore, to introduce the basic agenda of the prose writer, sounding many of the principal themes and motifs which will appear in the prose narratives of cc 11-20. At the same time, the Temple Sermon is fashioned to accord with the broader purpose of the poetry of cc 2-10, that is, to exhort the nation to repent and to threaten them with disaster for failure to do so. As a unit the Sermon does not yet assume disaster nor does it pay any direct heed

---

[43] 7:6, 18. Cf., 11:4; 13:10; 16:11; 19:13.
[44] 7:8. Cf., 11:13-17; 19:4.
[45] 7:31. Cf., 19:5.
[46] 7:22. Cf., 11:7-8; 16:11-12.
[47] 7:21, 25. Cf., 11:4, 7.
[48] 7:24, 26. See below.
[49] 7:24. Cf., 11:8; 13:10; 16:12; 17:23; 18:12; 19:15.
[50] 7:25. Cf.
[51] 7:16. Cf., 11:14; 14:11.
[52] 7:34. Cf., 16:9.
[53] 7:20. Cf., 15:13-14; 17:4, 27, but see text-critical notes.
[54] 8:2. Cf., 16:4; 19:7.
[55] 8:2. Cf., 16:6.
[56] 7:31-33. Cf., 11:7-8; 19:6-9.

to the people's rejection of the message,[57] the tradition of which must surely have been available to the redactor. Its absence reinforces the interpretation above, that these chapter (cc 2-10) are designed to present the prophet's appeal to the nation as clearly as possible without embellishment or interpretation.

3. Structural Arrangement

Despite the presence of movement in the prophecy of cc 2-10 from a pleading, conciliatory tone to a more judgmental one, these chapters appear as a loose collection of material with only the barest structural outline. Efforts to uncover a clear literary arrangement in cc 2-10 fail consistently. In cc 5-10, however, the refrain of Yahweh's reluctant threat to punish his people (5:9, 29 and 9:9), the doublet of accusation against the false prophets and all the secure society (6:13-14 and 8:10b-12) plus the promise of attack from the North (6:22 and 10:22) form a sort of triple frame around the long prose interruption of the Prose Sermon creating this shape:

5:9, 29	Refrain: "Shall I not punish them for these things? says Yahweh; and Shall I not avenge myself on a nation such as this?"
6:13	Doublet: "For from the least to the greatest of them, every one is greedy for unjust gain . . ."
6:15	Threat of destruction from the North
6:22-26	Promise of destruction from the North.
7:1-8:3	Temple Sermon
8:10b-12	Doublet: "For from the least to the greatest . . ."
9:9	Refrain: "Shall I not punish them . . ."
10:22	Announcement of destruction from the North

This arrangement of materials in cc 5-10 suggests that the Temple Sermon may have been deliberately framed by two sections of material which make the same basic argument. Yahweh is reluctant to punish (the refrain), but all the society is guilty (doublet) and so punishment will come from the North. Sandwiched between this somewhat circular presentation of the prophet's message, the prose narrative of the Temple Sermon

---

[57]The prophet is merely warned that he will not be heard (7:27).

concerned with Israel's cultic abuses presents an urgent plea for the people to amend their ways.

In cc 2-10, therefore, the prophet's message appears in an episodic and circular fashion. The argument spirals around pleas for repentance and threats of judgment and it reaches a high pitch of destructiveness in the dirges of the women intoning the certain arrival of the assailant from the North (9:10ff.).

Absent from this presentation of the prophet's message, however, are several of the themes introduced in the call narrative of c 1 (see above). Neither the rejection of the prophet by the people nor the prophet's ultimate triumph is addressed in these chapters. The prose of 7:27 alludes to the former theme only obliquely and it appears nowhere in the poetry; the latter theme is simply omitted. Nor is its corollary, Yahweh's fulfillment of the word, directly considered. Only the threat of doom appears in that regard. Instead, cc 2-10 offer cascading images and circular arguments regarding only two themes of the first chapter, the people's idolatry and rebellion and the disaster boiling over from the North. The other themes of c 1 await address in cc 11-20.

C. Cc 11-20: The Rejection and Triumph
of the Prophetic Word

In cc 11-20 the texture of the Book undergoes a major change in comparison with that of cc 2-10. New forms appear, new thematic threads are introduced, and the material takes on a new structural configuration.

1. Form-Critical Components

Form-critically, there are three new features in the text. First, the proportion of prose to poetry is altered sharply in cc 11-20. Here, the amount of prose outweighs the amount of poetry, reversing the ratio of these genres found in cc 2-10. Second, prose accounts of symbolic actions of the prophet[58] appear here for the first time in the Book. Third, the

---

[58]Cc 13, 19 and, perhaps, 16, 18 and 20 where symbolic activity occurs. Whether these accounts should be judged as a distinct literary genre is open to question. In each instance the symbolic activity performed either by the prophet (13, 19 16) or by another (18 by the Potter, 20 by Pashur but see below), becomes the occasion for a prose sermon which interprets the action and is cast in the same style as the rest of the prose sermons in cc 11-20.

most important new formal ingredient from the viewpoint of this study, the confessions occur exclusively in these chapters.

2. New Thematic Components

The new thematic threads and emphases in cc 11-20 parallel the changes in the literary forms of cc 11-20. First, pleas for the people to amend decrease sharply in these chapters, occurring only once in the poetry (13:15-17) and twice in the prose (17:19-27 and 18:12). Second, the accounts of the symbolic activities of the prophet (and of others) heighten the impact of the prophet's proclamation. No longer is the prophet's message simply a spoken word; now it is also an enacted word dramatically appealing to the people through a new medium.[59] Third, the addition of the confessions to cc 11-20 also adds the new thematic ingredients of the persecution of the prophet and his requests for vindication. (See above.)

In c 20, Lindblom, *Prophecy in Ancient Israel*, 169, finds symbolic action in Jeremiah's naming of Pashur and in this he is correct, but of far more importance symbolically is the action done to the prophet by the priest (see below).

According to Lindblom, a symbolic action is a symbol which points beyond itself to something else, "an acted simile," "*verbum visible*." To be genuine, a symbolic action must possess intentionality and historicity (168-173). But Lindblom is overly concerned with the prophet's psychology and his criteria are too narrow. While symbolic activity may have been recorded from true historical memories about the prophet, they might easily indicate later stages of reflection on the message of the prophet. There is insufficient evidence to make this judgment. This study is more concerned, therefore, with the function of these symbolic activities within the text.

[59]Lindblom, *Prophecy*, 178, suggests correctly that the symbolic activities function to warn the people that the predicted events will indeed happen. It is perhaps not coincidental that the three invitations to amend found in cc 11-20 occur in close association with Jeremiah's symbolic activity. The poetic plea for amendment (13:15-17) follows closely upon the account of the destruction of the linen waistcloth (13:1-11); the prose appeal of 17:19-27 precedes the visit to the potter's house and the summons to repent of 18:11 follows upon the account of that visit. The visit to the potter's house, therefore, is framed by such invitations to amend, a literary device the significance of which will appear below. At this point in the argument, however, it can be asserted confidently that this close association of the two types of material has the effect of increasing the urgency of the prophet's message.

The response of the people to the prophet becomes an important interest of the Book for the first time.

Cc 11-20, therefore, are characterized by new and more varied form-critical components which correspond to a heightened urgency in the prophetic traditions found there. Less attention is given to the prophet's poetry (his *ipsissima verba*) and more is given to interpretive comment of the prose.

3. *New Structural Arrangement*

The following description of the content of cc 11-20 demonstrates that these chapters are composed of five units or collections of material; that although these collections are episodic in character, they do, nonetheless, manifest some evidence of literary arrangement; that the movement forward among these units is created by the dispersal of the confessions through the chapters and by the narrative thrust of the tightly composed cc 18-20; that the final audience for whom these chapters were composed was probably the people in Exile who needed an explanation of the Nation's Fall and hope for the future.

The materials of cc 11-20 are arranged in five broad divisions or collections of material according to the following schema:

a. Cc 11-12   *Curse*
                Collection of material on the theme of
                    Yahweh's Chosen.
                            Confession

b. C 13   Symbolic Action
                Appeal for Repentance
                Collection of material on the destruction of the
                    Proud

c. Cc 14-16   Collection of Materials on the End of Life in the Land
                    C 14   End of Physical Life
                    Cc 15-16   End of Social Life
                            Confession

d. C 17   Collection of Materials on the Heart which Yahweh will
                Judge
                            Confession

                                                  Confession
  e. Cc 18-20   Climax and Conclusion
                   Appeal for Repentance
                                                  Confession
                   Symbolic Action
                   Imprisonment of the Prophet
                                                  Confession
                   Curse

   W. Holladay has observed that cc 11-20 have been set apart from the
preceding and subsequent materials by a frame of curses (11:1-14 and
20:14-18).[60] He has also pointed out that the expression ארור האיש אשר of
11:3 appears in 20:15 as well. In addition to serving as an element of the
literary frame around the larger unit (11-20), the curse of 11:1-14 sets the
ominous opening score for these chapters.[61] The curse assures the people
of Israel that if they fail to listen, they will lose the Land. The literary
importance of the curse is underlined by the conspicuous absence of the
expected blessing upon those who listen to the covenant. (See Chapter 7.).
In its starkness this curse foreshadows all that will befall the nation by
the time the next curse is issued at the end of c 20.

a. Cc 11-12

   The opening prose narrative (11:1-14)[62] functions as the introduction to
the units of both cc 11-12 and cc 11-20. It exhibits the following
arrangement: Yahweh orders Jeremiah to issue the curse upon those who
refuse to listen (שמע) to the words of the covenant, and the special status
of Israel as Yahweh's chosen is described (vv 1-5). Yahweh commands
Jeremiah to exhort the people to heed the covenant. The people's past
failures are stated and their consequences described (vv 6-8). Because the
people fail to keep the covenant in the present time (vv 9-14), Yahweh
refuses to listen to either the people or the prophet.[63]

---

[60]Holladay, *Architecture*, 160-162.

[61]Holladay is not as clear on this point since his focus is solely linguistic.

[62]See Chapter 7 for a description of the formal components of cc 11-12.

[63]Robert R. Wilson in *Prophecy and Society in Ancient Israel* (Philadelphia: Fortress, 1980) 238, is undoubtedly correct in claiming that Yahweh's prohibition of intercession by Jeremiah (11:14; 14:11; cf., 15:1)

An intervening oracle (11:15-17) in which Yahweh promises destruction upon beloved Israel separates the confession from the narrative. Then the confession returns the chapter's focus to the intransigence of the people (11:18-12:6). It opens with a portrayal of the enemies' conspiracies (11:18-20) motivated, according to the redactional vv 21-23, by their rejection of his prophecy. (See Chapter 1.) Besides illustrating the people's sinfulness, the confession presents the first petition of the prophet to the Just Judge for vengeance against their mutual enemies (11:20, 12:3) and, simultaneously, indicts the Judge for lapses in the execution of justice (12:1-3). This confession, therefore, introduces themes which will recur throughout the unit of 11-20.

But for whom besides the prophet (see Chapter 6) are these themes important? If the Book's audience is in Exile as this study has been suggesting, surely the people already knew that the prophet's words had been fulfilled and that Yahweh's justice had prevailed. But this same audience did not interpret its circumstances as the execution of Yahweh's justice. The Deuteronomistic History makes this sufficiently clear. Theological explanations of the nation's demise were needed. The confessions' account of the nation's rejection of its prophet contributes to an explanation of the catastrophe.

Furthermore, the validity of the prophet's words would be a pressing question during the Exile for the Book contains not only words of Exile and judgment but also promises of hope, salvation and return. If Jeremiah had correctly proclaimed Israel's cataclysmic fate, Jeremianic traditions would be equally correct in proclaiming its future salvation. In such a view, the theological issues raised by the first confession and each subsequent one have much bearing upon the proposed audience of the Book. The original purpose of the confessions appear to have been broadened in this setting from the defense of Jeremiah's prophecy to the justice of God in dealing with the nation. Will Yahweh's justice prevail? Yahweh's response at this point in the Book is that things will only get worse (12:5-6).

So far cc 11-12 have argued that Yahweh would be thoroughly justified in destroying the nation because of Israel's perversity toward the prophet

---

was designed to portray Jeremiah as successful within the expectations of the Ephraimitic understanding of prophecy. Within this Ephraimitic perception, the role of the prophet was to intercede for the people to avert disaster. Jeremiah does intercede in 14:13 and 15:18, and hence, his failure to prevent the disaster required an explanation. The exoneration provided by the prose writer is that Israel was so sinful and so utterly unwilling to listen that Yahweh responded in kind.

and his God. In response to Jeremiah's question of 12:4, "How long will the land mourn?", Yahweh blames the plight of the land upon Israel's rebellion and upon the perversity of its leaders and again promises destruction (12:7-13). Thus the unit (cc 11-12) offers an explanation of the fall of the nation drawn from the prophet's poetry (11:15-16; 12:7-13), from his experience of personal rejection (11:18-12:6) and from the interpretive comments of the prose writer (11:1-14, 17, 21-23).

But, surprisingly, the unit does not end here but in words of hope for a mysterious future in which the fall of Jerusalem is an assumed reality (12:14-17). This prose narrative is carefully joined to the rest of cc 11-12 by the employment of נחלה in vv 14 and 15, by שמע in v 17 and by reference to בעל in v 16. Moreover, it is significant that the language of v 10 of the call narrative is given prominence here: נתשם, אתוש, v 14; נתשי, v 15; ונבנו, v 16 and נתשחי, נתוש and אבד in v 17. This linguistic repetition suggests that the same hand and/or same intentions are at work in both passages.

The variation from judgment to promise admits of several explanations. Jeremiah may have uttered the promise of salvation himself or it may have come from the preservers of the tradition. To understand this passage as the work of the prophet presents a number of difficulties. First, the text is prose not poetry. Second, finding an appropriate setting in the life of the prophet is not without problems. If the message of hope formed part of his original prophecy before the nation's fall, the power of his accusations against the complacency of the people would have been sorely diluted. Jeremiah would have resembled the false prophets speaking "Peace, peace when there is no peace." His urgent, often violent poems designed to shock and so to convert would have been rendered impotent by the elements of promise.

If a date after the capture of Jerusalem is projected for the prophet's delivery of this message, conflict arises with other narratives. In the passage under consideration, however, Israel's enemies are perceived as evil, contradicting Jeremiah's usual presentation of them, and they are offered a conditional salvation (12:14). That difficulty leaves only the time after Jeremiah has been carted off to Egypt by these same people who still refuse to believe that Babylon is serving as Yahweh's instrument of discipline. The Egyptian setting seems an equally unlikely one for this message because it is hard to assign a purpose to such a text in the Egyptian circumstances.

Far more light is shed upon the passage by supposing that it derives from an Exilic editor who arranged cc 11-12 to provide the full-range of God's message of salvation. That is, he elaborated and re-interpreted

Jeremiah's message for the new circumstances of Israel. First, he justifies the destruction of the nation by showing the people's intransigence (11:1-14), Yahweh's warnings (11:15-17 and 12:8-13) and the people's persecution of the prophet (11:18-12:6). But then he adds a word of hope which updates the prophet's message promising the salvation and judgment of Yahweh to all nations (12:14-17).[64]

If this assessment of cc 11-12 is correct, the first unit of cc 11-20 contains, in a proleptic manner, the whole plan of salvation for the nation, even as the Book itself progresses toward the brutal facts of the curse alone. Implicitly, the confession pleads for the fulfillment of that curse and, paradoxically, accuses Yahweh of failure to do so.

b. C 13

Alone of the five units of cc 11-20, c 13 lacks a confession. But the first symbolic action of the prophet and the last poetic exhortation to repent[65] appear in it. The significance of the latter observation is that Jeremiah's own preaching as recorded in cc 11-20 becomes increasingly hopeless about changing the nation's headlong course toward obliteration.

The chapter can be divided into the following components:

13:1-11,   a prose account of the symbolic action and an interpretive
           sermon;
vv 12-14, a prose threat of judgment;
vv 15-27, a collection of oracles of the destruction of Israel's
           pride.[66]

In this second unit, the symbolic destruction of the waistcloth provides the occasion for an interpretive prose sermon. Told in the first person and recording commands of Yahweh to the prophet (vv 1, 4, 6), this narrative resembles the prose sermon of 11:1-14 in structure, in language and in content.

Structurally the passages are similar. Jeremiah receives commands from Yahweh (11:2, 6 and 13:1, 3, 6); Jeremiah receives a message from

---

[64]The latter theological insight is usually understood to have received its fullest expression during the Exile. See Second Isaiah.

[65]Prose invitations to repent occur in cc 17 and 18. See below.

[66]Vv 15-17; 18-19; 20-27 are connected with the prose narrative by the pride-humiliation motifs in vv 8, 15, 17, 18, 20, 26.

Yahweh (11:3-5 and 13:8-11) and the nation's response is reported (11:9-10 and 13:10; see Chart below). Linguistically, the accusation against Israel in 13:10 recalls 11:13: "stubbornness of evil hearts," refusing "to hear my words," "gone after other gods to serve and worship them." In content, 13:1-14, like 11:1-14, appeals to Israel's special status before Yahweh and reports its willful rejection of that status. Because of its pride Israel will become like the ruined waistcloth—useless. The basis of the analogy between Israel and the cloth lies in more than the threat of destruction to both. Israel's nature was to cling to Yahweh in the same way a waistcloth clings to the loins (13:11), but Israel refused to listen שמע, 13:11).[67]

The juxtaposition of the narrative threats of judgment with the poetic exhortation to repent while there is still time (vv 15-17) indicates that the former are probably warnings to persuade the people to repent rather than affirmations of certain disaster. In c 13 there is still hope. Despite a gloomy prognosis for Israel (23, 27), it can still be saved in the eleventh hour if it repents in time (13:16).

The combination of materials in this unit makes an argument similar to that of the preceding chapter, circling the same themes in different imagery. Israel is special to Yahweh (13:11; 17c) but Israel has rejected its special status and so destruction is deserved (13:9, 19, 20, 24, 16). But rather than looking for future hope as in 12:14-17, a flicker of hope remains in the present, if only Israel could change its ways.

c. Cc 14-16

1. 14:1-15:4: The Drought. At first glance, c 14 seems to form the third unit of cc 11-20 all by itself, but c 14 is the first element of the larger topical unity of cc 14-16. (See Chapter 2.) Together these three chapters are concerned with the effects of sin upon Israel's physical and community life. C 14 focuses on the end of physical life in the drought-stricken nation. Containing neither a confession nor a symbolic action, the chapter comprises the following pieces:

---

[67]The brief sermon (13:12-14) added to 13:1-11 has no intrinsic connection with it except for its concern with judgment and destruction. In a new metaphor the expected filling of jars with wine after a full harvest becomes, instead, a filling of the inhabitants with drunkenness and destruction.

vv 2-6,   a poetic dirge on the effect of the drought on the land and
             its inhabitants;
vv 7-9,   a communal psalm of lament appealing to Yahweh for
             intervention;
vv 10-16,   rejection of the community's prayer by Yahweh in poetry
             (v 10) and in prose dialogue (11-16);
vv 17-18,   a poetic lament of the prophet (or Yahweh);
vv 19-22,   the communal psalms of lament continued;
15:1-4,   second rejection of the community's petition by Yahweh.[68]

The opening poem vividly depicts the impact of the drought. Even the
animals abandon their offspring for lack of life-sustaining water (14:5). In
the communal lament which follows, Yahweh is addressed ironically as the
מקוה of Israel, the hope and wellspring of Israel, an image which echoes
the broken cistern passage of 2:13. Similar language appears in the second
liturgical piece of this chapter (19-22). The verb form of קוה is used in
v 19 where the people proclaim that they "waited in hope" for peace
(נקוה) and in v 22, where they claim to "wait in hope" for Yahweh to act
נקוה. The repetition of this root, the presence of the communal lament
form, similar appeals to Zion theology (vv 9 and 19) and calls in Yahweh's
name (vv 9 and 21) suggest that the two pieces were an original unity now
separated by vv 10-16.[69]

Both liturgical appeals for help receive responses from Yahweh. V 10 is
an oracle of judgment which informs the people that they are being
rejected by Yahweh. The prose dialogue in vv 11-16 can be understood as
a continuation of the first refusal of the people's petition. Again Jeremiah
is told not to intercede[70] and a triple judgment is promised by sword,
famine and pestilence (v 12). But the prophet does intercede in vv 13-15
and he blames the people's circumstance upon the misbehavior of the
prophets. Yahweh disavows any connection with these prophets and
threatens destruction upon them and their listeners. Once again in the
prose, the issue is the people's relationship to Yahweh's word. They have

---

[68]See Rudolph, *Jeremia*, 102, for a similar opinion.

[69]Against Rudolph, *Jeremia*, 102 who argues that the expressions are
stronger in 19-22 than in 7-9, but this observation is surely debatable (see
v 9). Even if his contention were true, however, increasingly strong imagery does not require the introduction of a new piece. It probably represents the strengthening of the people's petition within the same poem.

[70]See note 62 above for an interpretation of the prohibition.

listened to a false word and so, they, along with the prophets, deserve death.[71]

The second refusal of the people's petition for release from the drought occurs as the bridge passage between cc 14 and 15 (15:1-4). Here Yahweh emphatically rejects all intercession for the people, even by the great prophets of the past (15:1). The three-fold destruction promised in the first response to the people's plea is repeated and expanded; a fourth disaster awaits Israel, captivity will be part of their punishment (15:2). The source of their trouble is also expanded from false prophecy (14:13-16) to include the failed kingship of Manasseh (15:4).

Though c 14 contains no symbolic act of the prophet, the drought itself functions as a symbolic condition or portent of the future. The land is uninhabitable because of the people's sin and, by implication, they do not deserve to live in it. Though the individual pieces in this chapter may have had a distinct identity before being combined here,[72] their present juxtaposition creates a literary structure in which the absence of a future in the land is revealed metaphorically.

2. *Cc 15-16: The End of Community Life.* The theme of prophetic intercessions helps to unify c 15 (15:1-4, 5, 19. See above.) This theme highlights the hopelessness of Israel's situation, a hopelessness which is not mitigated by the oracle of judgment featuring the plight of the women (15:5-9). In it, all normal family life in the land is doomed. Similarly, in his second confession the prophet appears doomed (15:10-18). His life is cursed because of his prophetic vocation (15:16). He refrains from social life because of his vocation (15:17). His pain is incurable and Yahweh seems to have abandoned him (15:18) as Yahweh abandoned the people (14:8, 9, 19). In these hopeless circumstances, the prophet begs for vengeance upon his persecutors (15:15) and accuses Yahweh of treachery and infidelity (15:18).

Yahweh's response to the prophet (15:19-21) functioned originally as a means of validating Jeremiah as the true prophet who will meet Yahweh's conditions over against the false prophets who set their own conditions. (See Chapter 2.) In its present location the response of Yahweh to the

---

[71]See Nicholson, *Preaching,* 126.

[72]For example, the liturgical materials were probably used in worship before being joined with the prose and poetry here. With the exception of v 22, they make no reference to drought conditions. The prayer may have been used originally in connection with any community disaster.

prophet's complaint emphasizes, instead, the ultimate vindication of the prophet. Despite the darkness of his circumstances Yahweh will deliver him and fortify him against those who fight against him. This has the effect of setting the prophet's dismal circumstances apart from those of the people for whom no such future hope is provided. (But see below.)

The layered prose sermon of c 16 (vv 1-13, 14-15, 16-18) is based upon a midrash on 15:17. (See above.) In this meditation on the life of the prophet, his prophetic sufferings become a metaphor for what will soon afflict his people (16:1-9). But the interpreter is concerned primarily with the reasons for the approaching disaster. Three questions bring the reader to the point of the passage. "Why does Yahweh declare all this evil against us? What are our iniquities? What are our sins which we have committed against Yahweh our God?" (v 10). In the past and in the present Israel has forsaken its special status as Yahweh's chosen and gone after other gods (16:11-12). And, of course, Israel has refused to listen (16:12). Such is the testimony of the preceding confession (15:10-21). As a result the nation will be hurled from the land (16:13).

But the nation is not left entirely without hope. There will be a future created by a new Exodus event, not from Egypt but from the nations of the diaspora (16:14-15, cf., 23:7). After explaining why Israel was severed from the land (16:1-13), an editor wished to update the traditions by presenting the nation with an open future as he did in 12:14-17.[73]

A similar explanation can be offered for vv 19-21. These verses include a liturgical piece which foresees a day when all nations will recognize Yahweh's sovereignty. The prose v 21 interprets this liturgical prayer for the immediate context of c 16 by promising a mysterious action which will definitively reveal Yahweh's power.[74]

Between the two promises of future salvation (16:14-15 and 19-21), two further prose verses return the focus to the theme of imminent judgment upon Israel for its idolatry. The recalling of the nation's sin before the

---

[73]See note on 12:14-16 above. The formula לכן הנה-ימים באים is a tip-off to the eschatological nature of the prediction, and the new exodus motif is most at home in the Exile. See Rudolph, *Jeremia*, 112, and Isa 43:16-21. Whether this material is the work of the prose writer of 16:1-13 or of a later editor cannot be easily decided.

[74]It should be noted that this method of prose comment upon poetry is typical procedure in Jeremiah as observed in the study of the individual confessions (11:17; 11:21-23; 12:6; 18:18).

destruction of Jerusalem may also allude to the situation of the people during the Exile where idolatry always threatened.[75]

Cc 15-16, therefore, revolve around the principal theme of the end of social life in the land. The behavior of the people is such that all human intercourse, both physical and social, produces no fruit. Life in the land is cursed. The prophet also appears cursed. But he pleads for vindication through the fulfillment of the curse and is promised victory (15:10-21).

Together cc 14-16, the third unit within cc 11-20, present a gloomy and hopeless picture of Israel's relationship to the land. The curse upon those who do not listen to the covenant (11:1-14) is fulfilling itself. Neither the land nor the social structures can support life. The word continues to be rejected (15:10-21; 16:12) and the cataclysm looms as inevitable. So the main thread of cc 11-20 progresses toward an empty future.

Yet on another level, that of the audience of the Book, there is a new circumstance. The nation has met disaster. It has been scattered in Exile and it awaits a new intervention by Jeremiah's God. It awaits a future in the land of promise. Cc 14-16, consequently, end as do cc 11-12, with a promise of universal recognition of Yahweh's divinity.

d. C 17: Where is the Word of Yahweh?

C 17, really not aptly described by the word "unit," has successfully confounded scholars who attempt to find order or argument within it.[76] This collection of wisdom sayings (17:5-11), prose sermons (17:1-4; 19-27), a liturgical fragment (12-13) and a confession (14-18) offer, instead, scattered pieces of an unsolved puzzle. (See above.)

Two thematic assertions of this chapter deserve attention. The first is that the materials joined around the word לב make an important theological claim at this juncture of cc 11-20. Israel's heart is declared cursed in 17:5. The heart in general is declared corrupt and incomprehensible in 17:9. But in 17:10 Yahweh is proclaimed Judge who tests the heart and who administers justice. After having claimed in cc 14-16 that life in the land in all its forms is about to cease because of Israel's sins, the collector of c 17 affirms that Yahweh is a just judge who deals fairly with all. This claim is, of course, consonant with Jeremiah's confessions (11:20 and

---

[75]Hossfeld and Meyer, *Prophet,* 141.

[76]Holladay, *Architecture,* 151; Thiel, *Die Deuteronomistische Redaktion,* 202; and Rudolph, *Jeremia,* 112-119.

20:11) where he makes an appeal for vindication to the justice of this Judge.

The second important thematic ingredient of this chapter appears in the confession itself when Jeremiah quotes the mocking words of his enemies.[77] "Where is the word of Yahweh? Let it come." This remark of Jeremiah's enemies pinpoints a major concern of the Book to this point. If Jeremiah had been delivering a true word of judgment, why has it not been fulfilled? Cc 11-12 deliver a curse upon those who refuse a hearing to God's word; in its symbolic action, c 13 portrays the fate of Israel if it fails to repent in time; cc 14-16 depict the hopeless future for the people in a land without life; c 17 asserts that Yahweh is the Just Judge, but it also asks pointedly through the confession why justice is not being done. The confession, moreover, reports the rejection of the prophet by his enemies and his plea for the execution of justice (17:18).

This confession marks a shift in Jeremiah's tone of address to Yahweh. (See Chapter 3.) Yahweh is no longer accused of unrighteousness (12:1-3) nor of infidelity (15:18). Rather Yahweh is the One capable of healing the prophet, the one who is his praise (17:14), his "refuge in the day of distress" (17:17). As the people moved toward increased doubt in the prophetic word of Jeremiah, the prophet moved toward increased confidence in Yahweh's justice. Within the context of c 17, therefore, the confession serves to highlight the continued incredulity and stubbornness of the people as well as the mellowing and increasing confidence of the prophet. (See Chapter 6.) Furthermore the query of the enemies "Where is the word of Yahweh? Let it come." (17:15) also functions to foreshadow Israel's fast-approaching calamity. (See below.)

Before turning to cc 18-20, the prose sermon which concludes c 17 requires attention. This sermon contains the same formal elements of

---

[77] Again it is uncertain whether the prayer in 17:12-13 should be understood as the voice of the people or as the intercession of the prophet. See c 3 above for a discussion of the decision to view the verses as distinct from the confession. The expression "Yahweh is the place of our sanctuary," if understood as the prophet's prayer for his people, seems out of place. (Cf. 17:17 where Yahweh is the prophet's refuge against the people.) Perhaps this passage is a mocking representation of the people's hypocrisy. It borrows imagery from the Zion tradition and, if it functions like the other liturgical pieces in cc 11-20, should be understood pejoratively. The placement of the confession immediately after strengthens this interpretation. In 17:14 Jeremiah claims that Yahweh is his praise and asks for salvation for himself and not for the people.

prose narratives found elsewhere in cc 11-20. These formal components can be charted as follows:

11:1-14

2,6	Jeremiah receives commands
3-5	Message given
7-8	Ancestor's response
9-10	Nation's response

13:1-14

1,3,6	Jeremiah receives commands
8ff	Message given
10	Nation's response

16:1-13

2,5,8,10	Jeremiah receives commands
3,5b-7,9	Message given
11	Ancestor's response
12	Nation's response

17:19-27

19	Jeremiah receives a command
21-22	Message given
23	Nation's response

18:1-12

2,11	Jeremiah receives commands
6-10,11	Message given
12	Nation's response

19:1-15

1-3	Jeremiah receives commands
3,12-13	Message given
4-5	Nation's response[78]

In c 17 Yahweh commands Jeremiah to make an announcement (vv 19-20). The message is given (vv 21-22), the ancestor's response is described (v 23) and the conditions for permanent life in the city follow (vv 24, 26, 27). This structural similarity of c 17 with the other prose narratives in

---

[78]20:1-6 does not fit this structural pattern. See below.

cc 11-20 indicates that the c 17 prose sermon is from the same hand as the others.[79] Moreover, the language of 17:19-27 is typical of the formulaic prose writer.[80]

But in 17:19-27 the topic under discussion is a new one. Negatively, the people are commanded not to carry a burden on the Sabbath, and positively, to consecrate the Sabbath (vv 21, 22, 24, 27). Because this Sabbath concern appears contradictory of the thrust of Jeremiah's message in general and of the Temple Sermon (c 7) in particular, many scholars argue that, not only is it not Jeremianic, it is also not from the writer of the remainder of the prose sermons.[81] But the style and the language of this passage is so close to that of other prose sermons that this position cannot be maintained. In particular, the favorite theme of the prose material is repeated here: To the command to keep to Sabbath, the people would not listen שמע (17:23). If they persist in this refusal, the sermon warns them a holocaust will consume Jerusalem and all its inhabitants (v 27). But if they listen, the Kings will hold the throne of David and all Israel will worship in Jerusalem (v 26).

This passage and c 7 serve two different purposes. The Temple Sermon was designed to indict Israel for its cultic failures, its idolatry and to exhort repentance. (See above.) The Temple itself is not under attack. The point of assault is the bogus security the people find in the Temple despite their unjust and idolatrous behavior (7:4-11). From the perspective of the proposed Exilic audience, the Temple Sermon provides an explanation of the calamity of the Exile and serves as a warning against renewed idolatry in the land of Exile.[82]

The prose sermon of c 17 has a different concern, that is, to encourage proper cultic behavior on the Sabbath. Although the setting given in the text is Jerusalem, the passage is best understood as addressed to people who live outside the land and, hence, who are in need of the corporate and theological identity provided by Sabbath-keeping. The reward promised for obedience—restoration of national life in the land (17:25, 26)—lends probability to this interpretation. This prose sermon presents another

---

[79]See John Patterson, "Jeremiah," *PCB*, 468, who dates the text in the age of Ezra.

[80]Cf., vv 23, 24 and 27.

[81]See Weiser, *Das Buch*, 155 and Giesebrecht, *Jeremia*, 101.

[82]Cf., Isa 44:9-20.

instance of the prose writer's promises of hope to a suffering and punished people.[83]

Appearing at first as a confused melange of pieces, c 17 now appears to contribute important themes fo cc 11-20. It appeals to the Just Judge for judgment upon the human heart and, by means of the confession, it asks when that judgment will come. It softens the prophet's anger as the fulfillment of his prophecy approaches. And through the juxtaposition of the prose sermon and the confession, it emphasizes the failure of the people to heed Yahweh's word. But because it makes punishment conditional upon disobedience, there is still some small hope for conversion at this point in the narrative.

e. Cc 18-20

Alone of the five units in cc 11-20, cc 18-20 put forward a fairly tight narrative of events leading to the fulfillment of Jeremiah's prophecy.[84] In the prose narrative introducing the unit (18:1-12), a symbolic action takes place but it is not performed by the prophet. The action is that of a potter whose activity becomes the occasion for an interpretive sermon by the prophet. Yahweh relates to Israel as the potter relates to a piece of clay, that is, Yahweh can fashion the people in any way at all (18:5). In describing potential actions of Yahweh toward Israel, this sermon employs language borrowed from v 10 of the call narrative, but it applies it in a curious way. Yahweh declares he can pluck up (לנתוש), tear down (לנתוץ), and destroy (להאביד, 18:7), build (לבנת) or plant (לנטע) any nation or kingdom (18:9). What is peculiar about this is that the immediate context refers to only one nation, Israel.[85] Yet in this sermon the call language makes a universal claim regarding Yahweh's authority. Once again prose material within cc 11-20 presents theological claims which would be most at home during the period of the Exile.

The prose sermon of 18:1-12 marks the turning point in the story of Israel's fate recounted in cc 1-25. The last exhortation to repent appears here when Yahweh demands, "Turn back, each of you from your evil way

---

[83]See Bright, "The Date of the Prose Sermons," 23, for arguments assigning this sermon to the same date as the other sermons but for different reasons. He sees the material as "boggled" by the disciples and, hence, inconsistent with Jeremiah's Temple Sermon.

[84]See above for a description of the formal components of this unit.

[85]Cf., 12:14 where the same language is used for Israel's many evil neighbors.

and make good your doings" (18:11). The people answer with a dramatic and definitive no. "We will each follow our own thoughts and follow the stubbornness of our evil heart" (18:12). Henceforward in cc 1-25, there will be no more appeals to the people, no more flickers of hope. The remainder of cc 18-20 merely enacts the series of events which propel the nation toward destruction.

In a lament following the prose sermon, Yahweh expresses his incredulity that the chosen people have forgotten their God (vv 14-15) and have brought such a horrible fate upon themselves (vv 16-17). The fourth confession (18:18-23), placed at this climactic juncture of the Book, advances events further. It presents virulent petitions of the prophet for vindication against his enemies. Unlike the other confessions, this one consists almost entirely of petition (see Chapter 4) which, in the context of c 18, leads to heightened expectation of Yahweh's intervention. Moreover, no direct accusation is made against Yahweh in this confession. The prophet expects Yahweh to avenge him. He relies upon Yahweh's knowledge and control of circumstances (vv 19, 23) to produce a response.

Jeremiah does not have to wait long. In the third passage following the people's definitive rejection of Yahweh, Jeremiah's petition is answered (19:1-15). The breaking of the potter's flask before the official representatives of the people (19:1, 10), the second symbolic act of the prophet, proclaims and symbolizes the imminent destruction of the nation. The consequence of the breaking of the flask is that the divine judgment is set inevitably in motion. Through the prophet Yahweh announces "I am about to bring upon this city and upon all its towns, all the evil which I pronounced against it because they have stiffened their neck refusing to hear my words" (19:15). This summary sentence enables the prose writer to make his monotonous major point again. Israel refused to listen to Yahweh's word, a point illustrated by the preceding confession (18:18-23) and by the prose account of events at the potter's house (18:1-12). Israel had been warned. Yahweh had made every effort to turn them around. They deserved to become like the broken flask.

In 20:1-6, a prose account which is different in formal elements from the previous prose sermons,[86] new content is also introduced. For the first time in the prose narrative, the persecution of the prophet appears outside the confessions. The prophet is imprisoned and beaten by the chief

---

[86]This narrative also includes a sermon (vv 3b-6) but it lacks the commands of Yahweh to the prophet and a recounting of the nation's response. Compare with chart above.

priest of the Temple. In other words, the chief officer of Yahweh's house repudiated Yahweh's messenger and the message. Pashur "heard Jeremiah prophesying these things. Then Pashur beat Jeremiah and put him in the stocks . . ." (20:1-2).

Jeremiah uses his release from the stocks as an occasion for a sermon. In a play on words, Pashur's name is changed to מגור מסביב, an epithet hurled at Jeremiah by his enemies in the following confession (20:8). Rather than saving his people, Pashur has become a cause of their downfall by acting as a false prophet (20:6). His false word deafened them to the message of the true prophet.

Also, for the first time in the Book, the curse about to be fulfilled against Israel becomes precise. No longer is there reference to a mysterious threat from the North (1:13; 6:22; 10:22) nor to servitude in "a land you do not know" (15:14; 17:4), but the precise place of Exile, Babylon, is finally named.

This passage represents the climax of cc 1-25. All that has been suggested, threatened, warned against is about to occur. There are no more questions to be asked. There is no more hope of repentance to avert the cataclysm. Jeremiah's imprisonment in the stocks is a symbolic event. The word of God and its messenger are imprisoned in the Temple, just as the people are to be imprisoned in the land of Babylon. Ironically, for Jeremiah this is, at last, the moment of vindication.

The juxtaposition of the fifth confession with the event of his imprisonment makes the imprisonment the occasion of his hymn of victory. Alone of the five confessions, this one contains all the constitutive elements of the psalm of individual lament (see Chapter 5). As a result, the confession praises Yahweh, the Just Judge, for the justice about to be achieved (vv 11-13). Through it the prophet sings in praise that the word he has proclaimed (see 19:15) will be fulfilled. The flask has been broken (19:1-15) and Babylon is at the gates (20:1-6). The devastation of the nation is at hand just as the prophet promised from the beginning of the Book.

The prophet's curse upon his vocation closes the unit (20:14-18). To many scholars this text furnishes proof of the prophet's schizophrenia (see Chapter 5). Jeremiah has been vindicated, proleptically, at least, and confessed his joy in Yahweh's justice. Now he curses that vocation itself. But the placement of the cursing poem after the confession is not illogical for a number of reasons. First, along with the curse in 11:3, it frames cc 11-20. By the time the reader reaches c 20 the curse of 11:1-14 is about to be realized. The people have refused to listen to the words of the covenant, so according to the curse they are to be forced out of the land. The placement of the cursing poem at the end of c 20, therefore, creates a satisfying literary balance to the unit.

Second, it is not inappropriate to understand that, while the prophet rejoices in the confession at the vindication of his prophecy, he also despises the sin of his people and its consequences announced through his prophetic role. It is his own nation which is to be destroyed. Both the jubilation of the confession and the gloom of his curse are appropriate on the lips of the prophet at this point in the narrative. Third, the cursing poem, although clearly personal to the prophet, may also serve symbolically to foreshadow the fate of the people whose lives, along with his, will end in shame and sorrow.

D. Cc 21-25: The Aftermath

A brief look at the materials in cc 21-25 will confirm this interpretation of cc 18-20. Cc 21-25 function as an appendix to cc 1-20. C 21 reiterates the prediction of the Fall of Jerusalem to Babylon (21:1-7), but the Fall is treated as a *fait accompli* which introduces a new decisional problem to the community. The new problem is how to respond to the conquerors, not how to avoid the event itself. The famous chapters discussing the general failures of the institution of the monarchy (21:11-23:7) and the failures of the institution of prophecy (23:9-40) follow. These are succeeded, in turn, by a prose chapter concerned with another aspect of the new problem facing the community, the identification of the true Israel. Is the true Israel the exilic community in Babylon or the remnant in Judah? (c 24). The appendix concludes with a prose summary of all the main themes of the prose writer (25:1-14).[87]

The importance of this summary of cc 21-25 is that the shift in subject matter corresponds to new circumstances of the people. No longer is the problem the conversion of Israel. The dilemma facing the people is how to cope with and explain the disaster which has already occurred. The survivors are instructed to adjust to this new political circumstance by bestowing their loyalty upon Babylon, and they can find an explanation of their

---

[87] In this summary, the following themes appear: the persistence of prophetic warning to Israel (v 3); the people's refusal to listen to the prophet (vv 4, 7, 8); command to repent of idolatry (vv 5-6); proclamation of judgment at the hand of Babylon (v 9) and of the end to life in the land (vv 10-11); and an announcement of future punishment against Babylon (vv 12-13).

collapse as a nation, to some extent at least, in the failure of their leadership.

Cc 21-25 mark a shift in content from cc 1-20 where the problem is expressed in indictment, pleas for conversion and threats of punishment. Cc 21-25 offer instructions for surviving the disaster. This recognition that the tragedy has already occurred adds strength to the interpretation of cc 18-20 above. Cc 18-20 bring to a symbolic conclusion all the proclamation that has come before in the Book.

The argument of cc 11-20 may be summarized this way. Of the five units in cc 11-20 only cc 18-20 exhibit a tight narrative structure. Each of the previous units circles about themes in an episodic manner. The first unit, cc 11-12, announces the curse and describes Israel as Yahweh's chosen who willfully rejects the special character of its relationship with Yahweh. C 13 repeats this theme with different imagery and includes an invitation to repent before time runs out.

The content changes in cc 14-16. In these chapters there is less indictment and accusation and more attention is given to the consequences of Israel's sin. Life in the land will end. C 17 presents Yahweh as the Just Judge who will bring justice. But the confession of that chapter demands to see that justice. Cc 18-20 finally produce it. The final appeal to the nation to repent is rejected. With the symbolic smashing of the flask, the judgment is set inevitably on course. The prophet begs for vindication and receives it in c 19. In c 20 the prophet is imprisoned; Babylon is identified as the place of exile and the prophet sings in triumphant vindication. Yahweh is Just and the word is accomplished. The entire unit of cc 11-20 is then rounded off with the curse upon the prophet's fate as Israel is carried off to Babylon.

II. CONCLUSIONS

Cc 11-20, therefore, exhibit some literary structure. Across the length of them there is movement toward the fulfillment of the prophet's word. Moreover, within the five units of cc 11-20 there is an arrangement of material which intensifies the accusation, warning and threat of cc 2-10. But this observed literary arrangement cannot be pressed too far for, until cc 18-20, the four smaller units retain an episodic and incoherent quality, circling and repeating themes under new images rather than progressing linearly toward their conclusion.

Even the first two confessions (11:18-12:6 and 15:10-21), while carefully woven into their units, do not move the text forward. Instead, these poems contribute evidence of Israel's crimes in rejecting its prophet. The last three confessions continue to perform this function but with the third confessions (17:14-18) the question, "Where is the word of Yahweh?", accelerates the movement toward the fulfillment of the prophecy. Here the tightly structured cc 18-20 pull all the themes together and complete them. The people's rejection of Yahweh's word is irrevocable. The prophet begs for vindication (the fourth confession, 18:18-23). The flask is broken and the prophet imprisoned. Nebuchadrezzar approaches the city walls and the prophet proclaims his final confession in triumph (20:7-13).

The major themes of the call account not treated in cc 2-10 find their completion in this portion of the Book. Yahweh has faithfully watched the word to accomplish it (1:12); the metaphorical enemy from the North has arrived (1:13-16). Yahweh has been faithful to the persecuted prophet against whom the people did not prevail (1:18-19). The confessions play no small part in this broadening of the prophetic themes of the Book. It is these poems which provide evidence of the prophet's rejection and persecution and it is the final confession which celebrates his vindication. The third (17:14-18) and fourth confessions (18:18-23) hasten the narrative toward the destruction of the nation.

This means that the separation and dispersal of the confessions through cc 11-20 cannot be viewed as anything other than the deliberate activity of an editor. The separation of the confessions reveal a design which moves events toward climax and culmination. Cc 2-10 were arranged to present Jeremiah's poetic message of accusation and warning as plainly as possible. Cc 11-20 were shaped to portray the nation's rejection of that message (the confessions) even as the message was intensified and the appeal made more urgent (symbolic actions and cc 14-16) while the nation marched in headlong determination to its doom.

The prose writer summarizes this multi-layered message in 25:1-14 by blaming the people's plight (25:8-11) upon their refusal to listen to the prophet (25:1-7), but also by promising this people a new future in the mysterious freedom of Jeremiah's God (25:12-14). It seems logical to conclude from this that the prose writer, with his persistent accusation that the people did not listen to the prophet, would have been the one to incorporate the confessions into the Book for it is through them that we learn most graphically of their calculated rejection of the prophet to the nations.

9

Conclusions

I. THE COMPOSITION OF THE BOOK

To locate the conclusions of this dissertation within Jeremianic studies it is necessary to review the debate over the Book's composition in a fuller way than previously. At present almost every issue related to the composition of the Book—its date, author, setting and even the nature of the traditioning process—remains unsettled. The scholarly ferment over these matters can be divided into three stages.[1]

B. Duhm and S. Mowinckel inaugurated modern Jeremianic criticism with a three-source theory of composition that has, until recently, provided the major categories of the Book's interpretation.[2] In essence, their hypothesis claims that the Book comprises three written documents, A, B, C. Each derives from a different author and time period. The A source, Jeremiah's own poetry, is located chiefly in the early part of the Book. Authored by the eyewitness Baruch, the B source refers to the biographical narratives about Jeremiah found in the later half of the Book (cc 26-29, 34-44). The Deuteronomist wrote the C source, prose sermons and narratives of a highly rhetorical character scattered throughout the Book (for example, 7:1-8:3; 11:1-5, 9-14; 18:1-12). The Deuteronomist also compiled

---

[1]This division is more methodological than chronological since the last two stages overlap in current discussion.

[2]Duhm, *Das Buch*, X-XXI and Mowinckel in *Zur Komposition* and, with later minor modifications, in *Prophecy and Tradition: The Prophetic Books in the Light of the Study of the Growth and History of the Tradition*, Hist-Filos Klasse 3 (Oslo: I Kommisjon Hos. Jacob Dybwad, 1946).

the Book in its present form.[3] Accordingly, the Book's composition involved a complicated writing process. The articulation of this theory went a long way toward solving a number of problems in the interpretation of the Book such as the double accounts, the disordered chronology and the sudden variations in literary style.

Without challenging its assumptions, the debate's second stage fine-tuned the documentary theory of the first stage to accommodate it to the principles of form-criticism. For example, in their commentaries both John Bright and Wilhelm Rudolph accepted the tenets of the three-source theory, but both incorporated a more explicit theory of oral transmission into the process.[4] At this stage of the debate, most of the disagreement has been limited to the question of the authorship of C.

On linguistic grounds Bright rejected Deuteronomistic authorship, stirring up a scholarly controversy that is still not settled.[5] He contended that the rhetorical language of C was not uniquely Deuteronomistic. Instead, it represented the typical prose style of the seventh century B.C. This step allowed Bright to claim that the C materials were the work of Jeremiah's disciples who recorded "the gist" of the prophet's words. In contrast to the pejorative view of C's historicity postulated by source critics,[6] its reliability was now guaranteed.

Others have joined Bright in the rejection of the Deuteronomistic authorship of C. Moshe Weinfeld's[7] study of Deuteronomy claimed that both the Deuteronomistic corpus and the C materials contain formulaic language of neo-Babylonian and Assyrian treaties from the ninth to the seventh centuries.[8] Anyone writing prose at that time would have used similar language. Studying a narrow selection of texts, Helga Weippert[9] agreed. She proposed that this language was seventh century *Kunstprosa*

---

[3] *Zur Komposition*, 30. It was Mowinckel who emphasized the work of the compiler.

[4] Bright, AB, LXIII-LXXVIII and Rudolph, *Jeremia*, XIV-XXIII. See also the recent commentary of Thompson, *The Book*, 33-50.

[5] Bright, AB, LXVII-LXXIII and "The Date of the Prose Sermons of Jeremiah," *JBL* (1951) 15-35.

[6] Especially H. G. Mays, "Toward an Objective Approach to the Book of Jeremiah: The Biographer" *JBL* (1942) 139-155.

[7] Moshe Weinfeld, *Deuteronomy and the Deuteronomistic School* (Oxford: Clarendon, 1972).

[8] Thompson, *The Book*, 46, agrees.

[9] *Die Prosareden des Jeremiabuches*, BZAW 132 (Berlin: Walter de Gruyter, 1973).

(poetry without meter).[10] According to this line of thinking, Jeremiah himself could easily have been the author of C.

This is precisely where William Holladay takes the argument. In naming Jeremiah a possible author of C, Holladay attempts to preserve "the truth of the proclamation of the prophet Jeremiah."[11] This means that unless the prose sermons can be traced directly to the prophet, they are not reliable. So limited a view of biblical truth verges toward narrow historicism. But the most telling argument against Jeremianic authorship of C comes from Robert Carroll who asks if it is possible that the author of original, lyric poetry could be at the same time the author of bland, imitative prose.[12]

Jeremiah's authorship of C seems unlikely. Though one might claim that his poetry is derivative, e.g., he borrows motifs from other prophets, especially Hosea,[13] it is not imitative in the manner of the prose. In the poetry, Jeremiah dips into a common pool of prophetic imagery and genre, but, with the exception of c 2, he does not copy the oracles or the language of any prophet. Nor does he uniformly repeat his own imagery. Above all, his poetry is not rigidly formulaic; it is vivid, original and extremely concrete. The prose in cc 1-25, however, is the opposite. It repeats the same arguments in the same rigid formulae. It is lacking in concreteness and vivid imagery and much of it appears to be copied from Deuteronomistic literature. It cannot be the work of Jeremiah.

The third stage of the debate, characterized by traditions and redaction-criticisms, began with the tour de force of Claus Rietzschel.[14] Rietzschel argued that the Book was not composed of literary sources at all. Instead, it comprised oral tradition blocks,[15] arbitrarily piled next to one another by a redactor. Cc 1-24, for instance, include the following tradition complexes: cc 1-6 (the *Urrolle*); 7-10; 11-13; 14-17; 18-20; 21-24. The composition of the text, therefore, was an oral enterprise that took place in the synagogues of the Exile. The significance of Rietzschel's proposal lies in his recognition that the source-critical theory over-simplified

---

[10]Thompson, *The Book,* 46, uses the term "elevated prose."

[11]"A Fresh Look at Source B' and Source C' in Jeremiah," *VT* 25 (1975) 394-412.

[12]*From Chaos,* 9.

[13]Israel as a bride, 2:2, 7; Yahweh as provider, 2:9; Israel as harlot, 2:4, 4:12.

[14]*Das Problem der Urrolle: ein Beitrag zur Redaktionsgeschichte des Jeremiabuches* (Gütersloh: Gerd Mohn, 1966).

[15]*Überlieferung Blocks.*

the problems of the Book. Though his analysis did not bring the long hegemony of the source theory to an end, it seriously weakened it.

E. W. Nicholson continued the attack on the Duhm-Mowinckel position with his traditions study.[16] Nicholson also argued that the Book was produced by a long oral process, the final stage of which was conducted by Deuteronomistic tradents who adapted Jeremiah's message for the new circumstances of the Exile. The prose materials never existed as written documents nor can they be divided into two separate sources. They share a commonality of theme and purpose.

Nicholson's Deuteronomistic claims have not gone unchallenged. T. W. Overholt and J. M. Sturdy have both argued that the language of the narratives has as much in common with the Jeremianic poetry as it does with the Deuteronomistic literature.[17] Because unique Jeremianic vocabulary is used similarly in all levels of the tradition, Overholt denies the Deuteronomistic claims of Nicholson and nominates the prophet's disciples for the office of tradents. Sturdy also finds remarkable linguistic affinities between the prose and the poetry but argues that the same language is concentrated in only one chapter of the Deuteronomistic corpus, Dt 28. Sturdy concludes from this that Jeremiah's disciples were involved in some way with both Dt 28 and the Jeremianic prose.

Unfortunately, both investigations exhibit serious weaknesses. Overholt's study is limited to the word שקר; Sturdy's eliminates a number of Deuteronomistic phrases from consideration without sufficient warrant. These limitations notwithstanding, the combined linguistic investigations put Nicholson's Deuteronomistic theory in doubt. However, they do not refute his attack on the source-critical theory nor his fundamental assumption that the process of composition was an oral one.

G. Wanke,[18] another representative of the third stage of the debate, disputed the presence of the B source. He contended that the narratives in the second half of the Book are not a single, unified document authored by Baruch. Instead, they are three different cycles of material from three different authors among whom Baruch may be included. In Wanke's opinion, the three units are too diverse in style and viewpoint to permit their classification as a literary unit. Wanke differs from other scholars at

---

[16] *Preaching.*

[17] Thomas W. Overholt, "Remarks on the Continuity of the Jeremiah Tradition," *JBL* 91 (1972) 457-462 and *The Threat of Falsehood*; J. M. Sturdy, "The Authorship."

[18] *Untersuchungen zur sogenannten Baruchschrift*, BZAW 122 (Berlin: Walter de Gruyter, 1971).

this stage of the debate in his assumption that the compositional process was literary. For him, the prose traditions received their final form through the creative work of editors, not preachers.

As further evidence of the disagreement characterizing the discussion, Winfried Thiel's[19] redaction-critical study combines elements of both Wanke's and Nicholson's positions. With Wanke, he insists that the Book is a literary production. With Nicholson, he maintains that the final form of the Book is the work of the Deuteronomists.

Thiel finds evidence of the literary nature of the text in a stylized arrangement of the material in cc 11-20,[20] in the connective nature of some of the prose sermons in cc 1-25, and in the presence of the redactional connecting formulae in those chapter.[21] He derives evidence for the Deuteronomistic nature of the redaction principally from linguistic data. However, Thiel does not prove Deuteronomistic involvement; he merely asserts it, drawing on the alleged Deuteronomistic language to support his claims. Unfortunately, the linguistic data is too ambiguous and the argument too limited in scope to support his contention. Yet despite these weaknesses, Thiel's comprehensive exegesis of the text advances the debate methodologically by introducing redaction-critical assumptions into the center of the controversy.

Karl-Friedrich Pohlmann[22] follows Thiel's lead in another redaction-critical study. His aim is to uncover the literary goals of cc 37-44. These he finds in the fulfillment of promises of judgment against Judah issued in c 24. An investigation of that chapter reveals its literary, compositional character. From this Pohlmann concludes that cc 37-44 are redactionally related to c 24 as promise is related to fulfillment.[23] Pohlmann situates the redaction of the Book in Judah after the Exile because of the favorable orientation of cc 37-44 to the Babylonian Exiles. He speculates that the returned Exiles interpreted the Jeremianic traditions to establish their own dominance over those who remained in Judah. Pohlmann's analysis, therefore, joins Thiel's in claiming a literary character to the Book.

Clearly, the third phase of the debate has achieved more agreement

---

[19] *Die Deuteronomistische Redaktion* I.

[20] Ibid., 287.

[21] Ibid., 280-302.

[22] *Studien zum Jeremiabuch.* See also the earlier essay of Martin Kessler, "Jeremiah Chapters 26-45 Reconsidered," *JNES* 27/2 (1968) 81-88.

[23] The compositional character of c 24 is evident to Pohlmann in its linguistic and thematic dependence upon other texts. See *Studien*, 19-29.

about the demise of the source-critical theory than it has about proposing a satisfactory alternative. Scholars agree only that the poetic materials represent the actual preaching of Jeremiah and that the so-called B and C materials cannot be differentiated from one another with regard to purpose. Stylistic differences are explained as the joining together of different tradition complexes either during the oral stages or by deliberate literary activity. Scholars do not agree about the relationship of the prose to the poetry nor of cc 1-25 to the remainder of the Book. Nor can they decide the identity of the final redactors, the quality or quantity of their role, their setting or their date. And of importance for this study, they cannot determine the nature of the traditioning process which produced the Book.

Some argue that the traditioning process was primarily an oral one controlled by preachers. Others maintain that the traditions were transmitted by literary editors whose points of view are discernible in the text. This study aligns itself with the latter position because, in its analysis of cc 1-25, it has discovered a literary structure and a theological argument which cannot be explained by an oral transmissioning process alone.

Warrants for this claim come from a number of observations about the text. First, the call account in c 1 is a literary compilation. It functions as prologue to cc 2-25 introducing all the major themes: the sending of the prophet, the promise of judgment, the coming of "a foe from the North," the persecution of the prophet and the fulfillment of Yahweh's word.

Second, the distribution of the material between cc 2-10 and 11-20 confirms the operation of literary principles in the Book's composition. Cc 2-10 present the prophet's message in its starkness with little interpretation or commentary. The first three themes of the call account are introduced, invitations to amend are frequent and hope of repentance remains prominent. In contrast, cc 11-20 contain few invitations to amend, significantly increase the amount of prose commentary, decrease the amount of poetry, introduce symbolic actions of the prophet and contain all five confessions. Through new literary forms, cc 11-20 introduce and develop the two themes of the call narrative omitted in cc 2-10—the persecution of the prophet and the accomplishment of the word.

Third, the arrangement of the material in cc 11-20 reveals the work of an editor. The chapters are framed by curses making the fulfillment of the curse a major focus of the unit.

Fourth, the dispersion of the confessions throughout cc 1-20 provides a literary key to the enactment of the curse. They testify to the people's escalating rejection and persecution of the prophet, on the one hand, and to the prophet's growing certainty that he will triumph on the other.

Moreover, in their increasingly sharp petitions for vengeance (cf., 18:18-23), the confessions hasten the arrival of the curse.

Fifth, the placement and content of the tightly constructed narrative (cc 18-20) at the end of cc 11-20 also verifies literary activity in the creation of the text. These chapters follow closely upon the question of the enemies in the third confession, "Where is the word of Yahweh?", and they report succinctly the symbolic events of the curse's fulfillment.

Sixth, literary involvement in cc 1-25 is further indicated by the content of cc 21-25 and by the summarizing prose statement of 25:1-13. These chapters assume that the curse has fallen (cc 21 and 24), assign responsibility to the failed leadership (cc 22-23) and conclude with a summary of the Prose Writer's favorite themes.

Despite contrary claims of Rietzschel and Nicholson, literary activity in the production of cc 1-25 cannot be denied. The arrangement and distribution of materials, the development of the theological argument, the placement of the confessions and the unifying function of both the call account and closing summary show that the final form of cc 1-25 came from a writer.

At the same time, one cannot maintain that the Book is a pure literary distillation. Evidence of a complicated oral pre-history precludes such a judgment. First, the five units of cc 11-20 possess only limited thematic interconnections. Though a certain literary symmetry is present in their arrangement and a thread of argument runs across them, these features are not intrinsic to the material.

Second, with the exception of cc 18-20, the curses of cc 11 and 20 and the confessions, the rest of the units could be interchanged without greatly affecting the argument. For instance, cc 14-16, describing the end of life in the land, could be placed directly after cc 11-12, disturbing symmetry more than argument.

Third, the five units themselves offer a mixed picture of compositional history. Cc 13 and 17 possess only a loose inner cohesiveness created around the themes of pride and judgment of hearts. Cc 14-16 contain two originally separate sets of traditions (one on the drought, the other on the ill-fated women) now artificially connected. Yet within cc 14-16 there is evidence of literary dependence of c 16 on 15:17. Cc 11-12 are built around the theme of Yahweh's chosen but the prose sermon (11:1-14) and the confessions are connected to it only by catchword. Cc 18-20 alone exhibit a clear literary shaping in their narration of the last words and actions of the prophet before the Fall of Jerusalem.

The literary structure and theological argument uncovered in this investigation cannot be dismissed as coincidence. Rietzschel and Nicholson overlook the mixed compositional character of the material because their traditions-critical methods do not provide access to the literary features of the Book. But cc 1-25 are not a pure literary creation as Pohlmann proposes for cc 37-44. Cc 1-25 were the end product of a complicated oral and written traditioning process. Jeremiah's poetry circulated in separate blocks of material. Later, the major prose passages and the separately circulating confessions were incorporated, not as a random amalgamation of traditions, but in the literary scheme of a redactor.

This conclusion leads naturally to the further question of the identity of the redactor. In all probability that office was held by the Prose Writer. First, it was he who incorporated the confessions into the text to support and advance his argument. They are his illustrations that the people were given a chance to hear and obey Yahweh's word but they deliberately refused. Second, the Prose Writer used two confessions as texts for the development of two prose passages (16:1-13 and 20:1-6). Third, all major prose passages in cc 2-20 derive from the same hand and develop the same general themes (see Chapter 7). Their purpose is to adapt the prophet's message to a later audience. They exonerate Yahweh from the charge of injustice in the nation's collapse and they warn the people against idolatry and disobedience to Yahweh's word. These are theological issues of the Exile. Fourth, the same Prose Writer designed the call narrative of c 1 to introduce and unify the themes of cc 1-25. All these activities of writing, structuring and distributing the materials in cc 1-25 were the work of the Prose Writer-Editor who is the editor of cc 1-25.

Beyond identifying the redactor of cc 1-25 as the Prose Writer, no more can be said within the limits of this investigation. Too many questions remain to permit the establishment of the Prose Writer's identity or even setting. What relationship exists between cc 1-25 and cc 26-52? Is the same redactor responsible for arranging and attaching cc 26ff., and for composing other narrative materials in the Book? Are there several circles of redactors and traditionists at work in cc 26-52? Did the latter chapters undergo a different traditions-history from the former ones? These questions have not been adequately addressed in the literature and need to become the subject of a future study.

The relationship of the prose writer to the circle of Deuteronomists also lies beyond the scope of this paper. In many ways Nicholson's form-critical, linguistic and theological arguments for Deuteronomistic influence over the Jeremianic traditions converge in convincing ways, but the Sturdy and Overholt investigations press toward a modified view of this influence. The presence of much unique Jeremianic language in the prose materials suggests strong currents of continuity within the tradition. Yet neither study is conclusive (see above). The Deuteronomistic influence over the Book of Jeremiah may never be adequately explained, but it surely cannot be without more thorough language study and more satisfactory exegetical analyses of the whole text.

Nor can this study establish with any solidity the time or setting of the final redaction of the Book. The argument and exhortations of the prose writer seem directed toward the Jews in Babylonian Exile. Yet Pohlmann, in particular, has argued for a post-restoration Judahite redaction through which the Babylonian returnees established their hegemony over the competing Judahite and Egyptian factions. This may be true of cc 37-44 only or of the whole corpus. By itself this argument is plausible, but when placed next to the silence of the text on the restoration and the rebuilding of the Temple, the position is seriously weakened. In cc 1-25, at least, all reference to restored life in the land refer to some vague, idealized future with no concrete references to actual events of restoration. The burden of explanation of these silences falls to those who wish to understand the date of the Book as Post-Exilic.

II. THE INTERPRETATION OF THE CONFESSIONS

This study's interpretation of the confessions is perhaps of greater importance for Jeremianic studies than the modest contribution it makes to the compositional questions. This study has claimed that:

(1) The arrangement of the confessions as found in the Masoretic Text is basically correct.

(2) The psalm of individual lament form provides the structure for each of the confessions though it is fully present only in the fifth confession.

(3) Jeremiah creatively adapted this form to express his movement from ambivalence in his prophetic work to full confidence in his role as prophet.

(4) The cursing poem of chapter 20 is not a component of the last confession.

(5) The purpose of each of the confessions is to authenticate Jeremiah's vocation as a true prophet against the accusations that he was a false prophet.

(6) The appropriate setting for the original delivery of the poems is among Jeremiah's disciples.

(7) The purpose of the poems gives them a public, prophetic function explaining their preservation and collection with other prophetic materials.

158   The Confessions of Jeremiah

(8) As a collection of poems, the confessions move toward greater praise of Yahweh and certainty about the triumph of the prophetic word.

(9) The confessions were incorporated into cc 11-20 for literary and theological purposes
        (a) to illustrate the people's rejection of God's word in the person of the prophet and, hence, to justify the Fall of the nation.
        (b) to advance the movement of events by the prophet's intensifying cries for vengeance.

(10) The confessions were integrated into the text by a variety of literary devices but always in connection with a prose narrative.

(11) The one who incorporated the confessions into cc 1-25 was the Prose Writer.

(12) The Prose Writer compiled and arranged the introductory c 1, presented Jeremiah's undiluted prophecy in cc 2-10, reports the people's response and its consequence in cc 11-20 and compiled the aftermath in cc 21-25.

(13) Cc 11-20 possess a loose literary structure in which the confessions play a key role. Curses frame the chapters; each unit within reports the people's rejection of the word and the consequences of that rejection leading to the fulfillment of the curse. Cc 18-20 bring all these threads to a narrative conclusion.

These conclusions lead to a number of consequences for Jeremianic studies. First, the rearrangement or elimination of verses of the confessions in modern translations and commentaries is incorrect. These efforts to emend the poems according to preconceived psychological criteria fail to appreciate the confessions' literary form and purpose. Second, the confessions were preserved because they played a public, prophetic function in the life of Jeremiah. Psychological and biographical interest were not primary in their preservation.

Third, the confessions do not conclude with the prophet on the brink of despair. Jeremiah is not the Nietzsche of the Old Testament. His struggle with God his questions of theodicy, his complaints about his fate, all serve the same prophetic purpose—to establish him as a true prophet. The struggle ends in triumphant praise. Fourth, the traditional title "confessions" should be recognized as appropriate because it describes the theological purpose of the poems—to confess Yahweh's power over the wicked and the unjust.

Fifth, the Book of Jeremiah is not a random collections of oral traditions. There is a literary structure and an unfolding theological argument which cannot be explained according to the principles of oral traditioning alone. Cc 1-25, at least, went through the hands of a theological writer who gave shape and creative interpretation to the material.

III. TOWARD A HERMENEUTIC OF THE CONFESSIONS

Since the confessions existed in at least two different settings, the life of the prophet and the literary setting of the text, it is possible to speak of two levels of theological meaning.

In their original setting in Jeremiah's life the confessions are not transferable. They present his unique credentials as prophet, and so their meaning cannot be shifted to another individual or community. The emotional turbulence reported in the confessions is not the expression of universal suffering but is the specific suffering of the unwilling prophet.

At the same time, despite their unique original purpose, these splendid poems capture a human experience which has a universal quality about it. The innocent suffering wherein God becomes a deceitful spring, an unrighteous Judge, is an experience known to every generation of believers. In this experience, faithful ones are led through a dark valley to emerge renewed in faith and hope. This is what happens to Jeremiah, to the Suffering Servant and to Israel itself. In this light, the suffering of Jeremiah serves as a paradigm of the innocent suffering of believers. The confessions have been so prominent in Christian life and piety precisely because this is so.

In our time, Jeremiah's suffering and vindication holds special appeal. With particular ferocity in the twentieth century, small and large groups of people are victimized and oppressed by persons in power within their social group and by larger dominant cultures. The holocausts of the twentieth century raise Jeremiah's questions anew. Why do the wicked flourish? Are you not a Righteous Judge? Where is the word of the Lord? Though they arise from a specific set of historical circumstances, Jeremiah's questions are not unique to him.

Nor is Jeremiah's breakthrough from despair and loss of meaning to hope and trust in God's justice an isolated experience. Indeed, this feature of Jeremiah's confessions captures the repeated claims of the biblical testimony and presents a common, although not inevitable, pattern of human life within and without the Judeo-Christian tradition. That is, just at the point of deepest despair the one who turns toward the transcendent discovers profound new meaning and recognizes afresh God's salvific presence.[24] In the unique predicament of his historical circumstances, Jeremiah's confessions illuminate this common path.

The question of the justice of God receives an enlarged response in the confessions' new literary context of cc 1-25. Their original theme of theodicy is used by the redactor in a reverse manner to illustrate why the curse against the nation had to be enacted. The people rejected the prophetic word. Not only is God faithful to the prophet in the confessions, at the redactional stage that justice relates to the whole nation. In illustrating the intransigent deafness of the people, they proclaim the justice of God in destroying the nation.

That this apparent obliteration of all the promises of land and eternal covenant with David could be justice would have been a startling claim to those who were its recipients. According to Israel's traditions of land and kingship, the Exile demonstrated divine powerlessness not divine justice. For this reason, the argument of Jer 1-25 draws upon the conditional elements of the Mosaic covenant tradition to argue the reverse. In the Fall of the nation, Yahweh appears as the executor of the people's suffering, but it is the people who are responsible. They refuse to listen to the word of Yahweh and bring the curse upon themselves.

Such theological claims create problems for the contemporary believer. As a comprehensive explanation of human suffering cc 1-25 fail. But they do not attempt to offer such an explanation. Rather, they interpret a series of concrete events in the life of one nation at one point in history. In that set of events Yahweh was triumphant and faithful to the word announced through the prophet. That fidelity meant the punishment of the wicked and the defeat of evil in history. The punishment was neither arbitrary nor irrational.

The redactor's use of the confessions to justify Yahweh's sending of the people into slavery and Exile, therefore, should not be universalized to explain all tragedies of history. It should be recognized as a unique response to a specific set of evil circumstances. But what may be universalized, because it accords with the testimony of much of the rest of the canon, is that the just God's word will prevail against the evils of history. In this, the persecuted, the poor and the needy may take comfort and hope. The unpopular prophetic view of a wrathful God is, indeed, good news, for God's anger is an expression of divine intolerance of evil and of

---

[24]Such is the testimony of Augustine in his *Confessions*, Theresa of Avila, John of the Cross, Martin Luther, Thomas Merton, See, also, Ernst Becker, *The Denial of Death* (New York: Free Press, 1973).

divine love for the victims of wickedness.[25] The confessions sing praise of
God's involvement in human events on the side of the broken ones.

> Sing to Yahweh,
> Praise him.
> For he has rescued the life
>   of the needy
> From the hand of evildoers.

---

[25]For a discussion of divine wrath, see Abraham Heschel, *The Prophets*,
vol. 2, Harper Colophon Books (New York: Harper & Row) 59-78.

Bibliography

Ackroyd, Peter R. *Exile and Restoration: A Study of Hebrew Thought of the Sixth Century*. OTL. Philadelphia: Westminster, 1968.

Ahuis, Ferdinand. *Der Klagende Gerichtsprophet: Studien zur Klage in der Überlieferung von den alttestamentlichen Gerichtspropheten*. CTM 12. Stuttgart: Calwer, 1982.

Allen, L. C. "More Cuckoos in the Textual Nest: at 2 Kings XXIII.5; Jeremiah XVII.3,4; Micah II.3, VI.6 (LXX); 2 Chronicles XX.25 (LXX)." *JTS* 24 (1973).

Anderson, Bernhard W. "Exodus and Covenant in Second Isaiah and Prophetic Tradition." *Magnalia Dei: The Mighty Acts of God*. Edited by Frank Moore Cross, Werner E. Lemke and Patrick D. Miller. Garden City: Doubleday, 1976, 339-360.

Baumgartner, Walter. *Die Klagegedichte des Jeremia*. BZAW 32. Giessen: A. Töpelmann, 1917.

Behler, G. M. *Les Confessions de Jérémie*. Bible et Vie Chrétienne. Tournai: Casterman, 1959.

_____. "Vocation nenacée et renouvellée (Jer 15:10-11.15-21)." *La Vie Spirituelle* 560 (1969) 539-67.

Berridge, John Maclennan. *Prophet, People, and the Word of Yahweh: An Examination of Form and Content in the Proclamation of the Prophet Jeremiah*. BST 4. Zurich: EVZ, 1970.

Blank, Sheldon H. "The Confessions of Jeremiah and the Meaning of Prayer." *HUCA* XXI, 331-354.

_____. "The Curse, Blasphemy, the Spell and the Oath." *HUCA* XXIII/1, 73-95.

_____. *Jeremiah: Man and Prophet*. Cincinnati: Hebrew Union College, 1961.

Bredenkamp, V. J. "The Concept of Communion with God in the Old Testament with Special Reference to the Individual Laments and the 'Confessions of Jeremiah.'" Dissertation, Princeton University, 1970.

Bright, John. "The Date of the Prose Sermons of Jeremiah." *JBL* 70 (1951) 15-35.

_____. *Jeremiah*. AB 21. Garden City: Doubleday & Company, Inc., 1965.

_____. "Jeremiah's Complaint: Liturgy or Expressions of Personal Distress?". *Proclamation and Presence: Old Testament Essays in Honor of G. H. Davies*. Edited by J. I. Durham and J. R. Porter. Richmond: John Knox, 1970, 189-214.

_____. "A Prophet's Lament and Its Answer: Jeremiah 15:10-21." *Int* 28 (1974) 59-74.

Brueggemann, Walter. "Jeremiah's Use of Rhetorical Questions." *JBL* 92 (1973) 358-75.

Carroll, Robert. *From Chaos to Covenant: Prophecy in the Book of Jeremiah*. New York: Crossroad, 1981.

_____. *When Prophecy Failed: Cognitive Dissonance in the Prophetic Traditions of the Old Testament*. New York: Seabury, 1979.

Castellino, G. R. "Observations on the Literary Structure of Some Passages in Jeremiah." *VT* XXX/4 (1980) 398-408.

Chambers, W. V. "The Confessions of Jeremiah: A Study in Prophetic Ambivalence." Dissertation, Vanderbilt University, 1972.

Childs, Brevard. *Memory and Tradition in Israel*. STB 37. London: SCM Press, 1962.

Clines, J. A. and Gunn, D. M. "Form, Occasion and Redaction in Jeremiah 20." *ZAW* 88 (1976) 390-409.

_____. "'You Tried to Persuade Me' and Violence! Outrage!' in Jer XX 7-8." *VT* 28 (1978) 20-27.

Condamin, Albert. *Le Livre de Jérémie*. Paris: Librairie Victor Lecoffre, 1920.

Cornill, Carl Heinrich. *Das Buch Jeremia*. Leipzig: Chr. Herm Tauchnitz, 1905.

Crenshaw, James L. *Prophetic Conflict: Its Effects Upon Israelite Religion*. BZAW 125. Berlin: Walter de Gruyter, 1971.

_____. "The Human Dilemma and the Literature of Dissent." *Tradition and Theology in the Old Testament*. Edited by Douglas Knight. Philadelphia: Fortress, 1977.

Dahood, Mitchell, "Denominative riḥḥam, 'to conceive, enwomb.'" *Bib* 44 (1963) 204-205.

_____. "Hebrew-Ugaritic Lexicography IV." *Bib* 47 (1966) 409.

_____. "The Metaphor in Jeremiah 17,13." *Bib* 48 (1967) 109-110.

_____. "Philological Notes on Jer 18:14-15." *ZAW* 74 (1962) 207-209.

_____. "Two Textual Notes on Jeremiah." *CBQ* 23/4 (1961) 462-464.

Davidson, R. "The Interpretation of Jeremiah XVII 5-8." *VT* 9 (1959) 202-205.

Driver, G. R. "Jeremiah XII,6." *JJS* V/4 (1954) 177-178.

Duhm, Bernhard. *Das Buch Jeremia*. Tübingen: J. C. B. Mohr, 1901.

Ehrman, A. "A note on 'boteaḥ' in Jeremiah 12:5." *JJS* 5/2 (1960) 153.

Emerton, J. A. "Notes on Jeremiah 12:9 and some suggestions of J. D. Michaelis about the Hebrew words naha, 'aebra and jada.'" *ZAW* 81/2 (1969) 182-191.

Ewald, Heinrich. *Prophets of the Old Testament*. Vol. III. Translated by J. F. Smith. Edinburgh: Williams & Norgate, 1878.

Fohrer, Georg. "Neue Literatur zur alttestamentlichen Prophetie (1961-1970)." *ThRu* 47/2 (1982) 109-121.

_____. "Remarks on Modern Interpretation of the Prophets." *JBL* 80 (1961) 309-312.

Gemser, B. "The Rîb or Controversy Pattern in the Hebrew Mentality." *Wisdom in Israel and in the Ancient Near East*. Edited by Martin Noth and D. Winton Thomas. VTS 3. Leiden: E. J. Brill, 1955, 120-137.

Gerstenberger, Erhard. "Jeremiah's Complaints. Observations on Jer 15:10-21." *JBL* 82/4 (1963) 393-408.

Giesebrecht, Friedrich. *Das Buch Jeremia*. HAT. Göttingen: Vandenhoeck & Ruprecht, 1907.

Gordis, Robert, "The Biblical Root SDY - SD: Notes on II Sam I/21; Jer XVIII.14; Ps XCI.6; Job V.21." *JTS* (1940) 34-43.

Graf, K. H. *Der Prophet Jeremia*. Leipzig: T. O. Weigel, 1862.

Gunkel, Herman. *Einleitung in die Psalmen*. HKAT. Göttingen: Vandenhoeck & Ruprecht, 1933.

Gunneweg, A. H. J. "Konfession oder Interpretation im Jeremiabuch." *ZTK* 67/4 (1970) 395-416.

Habel, Norman C. "The Form and Significance of the Call Narratives." *ZAW* 77 (1965) 297-323.

Harvey, Julien. *Le Plaidoyer prophétique contre Israel après la rupture de l'alliance: Etude d'une formula litteraire L'Ancien Testament*. Studia 22. Paris: Desclee de Brouwer, 1967.

Hauret, Charles. "Jérémie, XVII, 14: *Sana me, Domine, et sanabor*," *RevScRel* 36/2 (1962) 174-184.

Hermann, Siegfried. "Forschung am Jeremiabuch Probleme und Tendenzen ihre neueren Entwicklung." *TLZ* 102/7 (1977) 481-490.

Heschel, Abraham. *The Prophets*. Two volumes. Harper Colophon Books. New York: Harper & Row, 1962.

Hillers, Delbert R. "A Convention in Hebrew Literature: The Reaction to Bad News." *ZAW* 77 (1965) 86-89.

_____. *Covenant: The History of a Biblical Idea*. Seminars in the History of Ideas. Baltimore: The Johns Hopkins Press, 1969.

Hitzig, Friedrich. *Der Prophet Jeremia*. KHAT. Leipzig: Weidmannsche, 1841.

Holladay, William L. *The Architecture of Jeremiah 1-20*. Lewisburg: Bucknell University and London: Associated Universities, 1976.j

_____. "The Background of Jeremiah's Self-Understanding: Moses, Samuel and Psalm 22." *JBL* 83 (1964) 153-164.

_____. *A Concise Hebrew and Aramaic Lexicon of the Old Testament*. Grand Rapids: William B. Eerdmans, 1971.

_____. "The Covenant with the Patriarchs Overturned: Jeremiah's Intention in 'Terror on Every Side' (Jer 20:1-6." *JBL* 91 (1972) 305-320.

_____. "A Fresh Look at 'Source B' and 'Source C' in Jeremiah." *VT* 25 (1975) 394-412.

_____. "The Identification of the Two Scrolls of Jeremiah." *VT* XXX/4 (1980) 542-567.

_____. "Jeremiah and Moses, Further Considerations." *JBL* 85 (1966) 17-27.

_____. "Jeremiah's Lawsuit with God: A Study in Suffering and Meaning." *Int* 17 (1963) 280-87.

_____. *Jeremiah: Spokesman Out of Time*. Philadelphia: Pilgrim Press Book from United Church Press, 1974.

_____. "The Recovery of Poetic Passages of Jeremiah." *JBL* 85 (1966) 401-435.

_____. "Style, Irony and Authenticity in Jeremiah." *JBL* 81 (1962) 44-50.

Hossfeld, Frank Lothar, and Meyer, Ivo. *Prophet Gegen Prophet: Eine Analyse der alttestamentlichen Texte zum Theme: wahre und falsche Propheten*. BB 9. Fribourg: Schweizerisches Katholisches Bibelwerk, 1973.

Houberg, R. "Note sur Jérémia 11:19." *VT* 25 (1975) 676-677.

Hubmann, Franz D. "Stationen einer Berufung: Die 'Konfessionen' Jeremias." *Theologisch-praktische Quartalschrift* I (1984) 25-39.

_____. *Untersuchungen zu den Konfessionen: Jer 11:18-12:6 und Jer 15:10-21*. FB 30. Echter: Echter Verlag, 1978.

Huffmon, Herbert B. "The Covenant Lawsuit in the Prophets." *JBL* 78 (1959) 285-295.

_____. "The Treaty Background of YADA." *BASOR* 181 (1966) 31-37.

Hyatt, J. P. "The Deuteronomic Edition of Jeremiah." *Vanderbilt Studies in the Humanities*. Vol. I. Nashville: Vanderbilt University, 1951.

_____. "Jeremiah and Deuteronomy." *JNES* 1 (1942) 156-173.

_____. *Jeremiah, Prophet of Courage and Hope*. Nashville: Abingdon, 1957.

Ittmann, Norbert. *Die Konfessionen Jeremias: Ihre Bedeutung für die Verkündigung des Propheten*. WMANT 54. Neukirchen-Vluyn: Neukirchener, 1981.

Janzen, J. Gerald. *Studies in The Text of Jeremiah*. Cambridge: Harvard, 1973.

Jüngling, H. W. "Ich mache dich zu einer ehernen Mauer: Literarkritische Überlegungen zum Verhältnis von Jer 1:18-19 zu Jer 15:20-21." *Bib* LIV/1 (1973) 1-24.

Kessler, Martin. "Jeremiah Chapters 26-45 Reconsidered." *JNES* 27/2 (1968) 81-88.

Klein, Walter C. "Commentary on Jeremiah." *AnThRev* LXV/2 (1963) 121-158.

Kraus, Hans-Joachim. *Psalmen.* BKAT XV/1. Neukirchen-Vluyn: Neukirchener, 1960.

Kremers, H. "Leidensgemeinschaft mit Gott in AT. Eine Untersuchung der 'biographischen' Berichte im Jeremiabuch." *EvT* 13 (1953) 122-141.

Limburg, James. "The root ריב and the Prophetic Lawsuit Speeches." *JBL* 88 (1969) 291-304.

Lindblom, J. *Prophecy in Ancient Israel.* Oxford: Cross & Blackwell, 1962.

Long, Burke O'Connor. "Two Questions and Answer Schemata in the Prophets." *JBL* 90 (1971) 129-139.

Lundblom, J. R. *Jeremiah: A Study in Ancient Hebrew Rhetoric.* SBLDS 18. Missoula: Scholars Press, 1975.

Loretz, O. "Stichometrie und Parallelismus Membrorum." *UF* (1962) 170-171.

McCarthy, Dennis J. *Old Testament Covenant: A Survey of Current Opinions.* Atlanta: John Knox, 1972.

McKane, W. "The Interpretation of Jeremiah XII.1-5." *GUOST* 20 (1964) 38-48.

_____. "Poison, Trial by Ordeal and the Cup of Wrath." *VT* 30 (1980) 474-492.

McNamara, M. "Jeremiah." *New Catholic Commentary on Holy Scripture.* Edited by Reginald H. Fuller, et al. London: Nelson & Sons, 1969, 601-624.

Marx, Alfred. "A propos des doublets du livre de Jérémie: Reflexions sur la formation d'un livre prophétique." *Prophecy: Essays Presented to Georg Fohrer.* Edited by J. A. Emerton. Berlin: Walter de Gruyter, 1980, 106-120.

Mays, Herbert G. "Toward an Objective Approach to the Book of Jeremiah: The Biographer." *JBL* (1942) 139-145.

Mays, James Luther. *Hosea*. OTL. Philadelphia: Westminster, 1969.

Meyer, Ivo. *Jeremia und die Falschen Propheten*. OBO 13. Göttingen: Vandenhoeck & Ruprecht, 1977.

Michelic, J. L. "Dialogue with God: A Study of Some of Jeremiah's Confessions." *Int* 14 (1960) 43-50.

Michaelis, J. D. *Observationes Philologicae et Criticae in Jeremiae Vaticinia et Threnos*. Göttingen: Vandenhoeck & Ruprecht, 1792.

Mowinckel, Sigmund. *The Psalms in Israel's Worship*. Two volumes. Translated by D. R. Ap-Thomas. Nashville: Abingdon, 1962.

_____. *Prophecy and Tradition: The Prophetic Books in the Light of the Study of the Growth and History of the Tradition*. Hist-Filos 3. Oslo: Kommisjon Hos Jacob Dybwald, 1946.

_____. *Zur Komposition des Buches Jeremia*. Videnskpsselskapets Skrifter 11. Kristiania: Kommisjon Bei Jacob Dybwald, 1914.

Muilenburg, James. "Form-Criticism and Beyond." *JBL* LXXXVIII (1969) 1-18.

_____. Jeremiah 1-20. Unpublished commentary. Two volumes. Speer Library. Princeton Theological Seminary. No date.

Müller, Hans-Peter. "'Der brunte Vogel' von Jer 12:9." *ZAW* 79/2 (1967) 225-228.

Nägelsbach, W. E. "The Prophet Jeremiah," *Lange's Commentary on the Holy Scripture*, 6. Grand Rapids: Zondervan, 1960.

Neumann, Peter K. "Das Wort, Das Geschehen Ist . . . Zum Problem der Wortempfangsterminologie in Jer I-XXV." *VT* 23 (1973) 171-217.

Nicholson, E. W. *Jeremiah 1-25*. CBC. Cambridge: University Press, 1973.

_____. *Preaching to the Exiles: A Study of the Prose Tradition of the Book of Jeremiah*. New York: Schocken Books, 1970.

Osswald, Eva. *Falsche Prophetie im Alten Testament*. SGVSGTR 237. Tübingen: J. C. B. Mohr, 1962.

Overholt, Thomas W. "Remarks on the Continuity of the Jeremiah Tradition." *JBL* 91 (1972) 457-462.

_____. *The Threat of Falsehood: A Study in the Theology of the Book of Jeremiah*. SBT 16. London: SCM Press, 1970.

Patterson, John. "Jeremiah" *PBC*. New York: Nelson & Sons, 1920.

Pohlman, Karl-Friedrich. *Studien zum Jeremiabuch: Ein Beitrag zur Frage nach der Entstehung des Jeremiabuches.* FRLANT, 118. Göttingen: Vandenhoeck & Ruprecht, 1978.

Rad, Gerhard von. "Die Konfessionen Jeremias." *EvT* 3 (1936) 265-276.

_____. *The Message of the Prophets.* Translated by D. M. G. Stalker. New york: Harper & Row, 1967.

_____. *Old Testament Theology.* Two Volumes. Translated by D. M. G. Stalker. New York: Harper & Row, 1965.

Raitt, Thomas M. *A Theology of Exile: Judgment/Deliverance in Jeremiah and Ezekiel.* Philadelphia: Fortress, 1977.

Reventlow, Henning Graf. *Liturgie und prophetisches Ich bei Jeremia.* Gütersloh: Gerd Mohn, 1963.

Rietzschel, Claus. *Das Problem der Urrolle: Ein Beitrag zur Redaktionsgeschichte des Jeremiabuches.* Gütersloh: Gerd Mohn, 1966.

Robert, Andre. "Jérémie et la Reforme Deuteronomique d'aprè Jer XI, 1-14." *Rech Sci Rel* 31 (1931) 5-16.

Rowley, H. H. "The Text and Interpretation of Jer 11:18-12:6." *AJSSL* XLII (1925/6) 217-227.

_____. *Men of God: Studies in Old Testament History and Prophecy.* London: Thomas Nelson & Sons, 1963.

Rowton, M. B. "Jeremiah and the Death of Josiah." *JNES* 10 (1951) 128-130.

Rudolph, Wilhelm. *Jeremia.* HAT 1,12. Tübingen: J. C. B. Mohr, 1968.

Schottroff, Willy. *Der Altisraelitische Fluchsprüch.* WMANT 30. Neukirchen-Vluyn: Neukirchener Verlag, 1969.

_____. "Jeremia 2:1-3: Ewagungen zur methode der Prophetenexegese." *ZTK* 67 (1970) 263-294.

Schneedorfer, Leo. *Das Buch Jeremias: Des Propheten Klagelieder und das Buch Baruch.* WKHSAT. Wien: Mayer, 1903.

Schreiner, J. "Unter des Auftrags aus der Verkündigung des Propheten Jeremias: Jer 11:18-12:6." *Bib Leb* 7/3 (1966) 180-192.

Selms, A. van. "Telescoped Discussion as Literary Device in Jeremiah." *VT* 26 (1976) 99-112.

Septuaginta: Vetus Testamentum Graecum auctoritate Societatis Gottingensis editum. XV: Ieremias, Baruch, Threni, Epistula Ieremiae. Edited by J. A. Ziegler. Göttingen: Vandenhoeck & Ruprecht, 1957.

Soggin, L. A. "Jer XII 10a: eine Parallelstelle zu Deut XXXII 8/ LXX." *VT* 8 (1958) 304-305.

Stone, P. F. "The Temple Sermons of Jeremiah." *AJSL* (1933/34) 73-92.

Stummer, Friedrich. "Bemerkungen zu Jer 12; 1-6." *MiscBiblOr.* Rome: Herder, 1951, 264-75.

Sturdy, John V. M. "The Authorship of the 'Prose Sermons' of Jeremiah." *Prophecy: Essays Presented to Georg Fohrer on his Sixty-Fifth Birthday.* Edited by J. A. Emerton. Berlin: Walter de Gruyter, 1980, 143-150.

Thiel, Winfried. *Die deuteronomistische Redaktion von Jeremia 1-25.* Two volumes. WMANT 41. Neukirchen-Vluyn: Neukirchener, 1971.

Thompson, J. A. *The Book of Jeremiah.* Grand Rapids: William B. Eerdmans, 1980.

Tov, E. "L'incidence de la critique textuelle sur la critique litteraire dans le livre de Jérémie." *RB* 79/2 (1972) 189-199.

Volz, Paul. *Der Prophet Jeremia.* KAT X. Leipzig: A. Deichert, 1922.

Wang, Chen-Chang. "A Theology of Frustration—an Interpretation of Jeremiah's Confessions." *SEAJT* 15/2 (1974) 36-42.

Wanke, Gunther, *Untersuchungen zur sogenannten Baruchschrift.* BZAW 122. Berlin: Walter de Gruyter, 1971.

Weinfeld, Moshe. *Deuteronomy and the Deuteronomic School.* Oxford: Clarendon Press, 1972.

Weippert, Helga. *Die Prosareden des Jeremiabuches.* BZAW 132. Berlin: Walter de Gruyter, 1973.

Weiser, Artur. *Das Buch des Propheten Jeremia.* Two volumes. ATD 20. Göttingen: Vandenhoeck & Ruprecht, 1952-55.

_____. *The Psalms.* OTL. Translated by Herbert Hartwell. Fifth revised edition. Philadelphia: Westminster, 1962.

Westermann, Claus. *Forschung am Alten Testament.* TBu 24. München: Kaiser, 1964.

_____. *Jeremia.* Stuttgart: Calwer, 1967.

_____. *The Psalms: Structure, Content and Message*. Minneapolis: Augsburg, 1980.

_____. *Lob und Klage in der Psalmen*. 5 auflage. Göttingen: Vandenhoeck & Ruprecht, 1977.

Wildberger, Hans. *Jahwewort und prophetische Rede bei Jeremia*. Dissertation #2. Zurich: Zwingli, 1942.

Wilhelmi, G. "Weg mit der vielen Altären (Jer 11:15." *VT* 25 (1975) 119-121.

Wilson, Robert R. *Prophecy and Society in Ancient Israel*. Philadelphia: Fortress, 1980.

Wimmer, D. H. "Prophetic Experience in the Confessions of Jeremiah." Dissertation, University of Notre Dame, 1973.

Wolff, Hans-Walter. *Hosea: A Commentary on the Book of Hosea*. Herm. Translated by Gary Stansell. Philadelphia: Fortress, 1974.

Index

SCRIPTURE PASSAGES

Authors